It is hard to problematize the familiar. With familiarity comes ...
which are entrenched in the minds of individuals, models which guide and make sense of individual behavior. The concept of luck is familiar to us all yet according to *Luck*, the word is a stranger to us all. I use it one way and you another. We disagree without ever knowing we do, and so our ignorance is never revealed. *Luck* has laid bare our ignorance and educates us on the concept of luck. *Luck* illustrates and explains how luck operates across a number of empirical contexts, highly familiar contexts in themselves. We need to reimagine the colloquialism that it is better to be lucky than good. If we judge research contributions like we judge Olympic dives, *Luck* receives top marks for degree of difficulty and execution.

—**Ray Reagans** *(Ph.D., Chicago), Alfred P. Sloan Professor of Management at the MIT Sloan School of Management, USA*

Understanding the powerful role of chance in human endeavors may be the most profound and revealing insights offered by scholarly study. Liu has written a sophisticated treatise on luck that offers something for everyone, including useful tips and scholarly insights too numerous to count.

—**Don A. Moore**, *Professor, University of California, Berkeley, USA and author of* Perfectly Confident

We all know that success in business, life, and sports depends in part on luck. But how do we hire, manage, make decisions, and invest in light of that fact? Do we seek out the best, or assume that they were just lucky? Do we fire our worst performers? Do we emulate successful people and organizations? In this surprising, captivating book, Chengwei Liu shows that the answers to these questions depend on the nature and magnitude of luck. We can, in fact, tell whether someone's been lucky or good. You no longer need fear being fooled by randomness. With Chengwei Liu's *Luck* as a guide, you can become a master of luck. You will learn to identify and quantify luck, and, most important, you will learn some counterintuitive strategies—such as hire the second best, fire the second worst, and never emulate the super successful. Learn this book and you no longer have choose whether you'd prefer to be lucky or good. You can be both!!

—**Scott E. Page**, *John Seely Brown Distinguished University Professor, Ross School of Business, University of Michigan, USA and author of* The Diversity Bonus *and* The Model Thinker

This book makes for a stimulating read. Written by a wonderfully original researcher, it encourages us to re-examine the prima facie evidence we rely on to make our choices. Moreover, in applying rigorous analysis, the author helps us understand the significance of luck in everyday life and, in doing so, encourages to take ourselves less seriously.

—**Mark de Rond**, *Professor, Cambridge University, UK and author of* There is An I in Team, The Last Amateurs, *and* Doctors at War

This book provides a magisterial survey of the concept of "luck" as well as practical ideas on how one can profit from it (or more precisely from other's beliefs about luck). Academics will find much to provoke thought, and managers will find insights that can help them rethink their strategies and craft new ones. And it is a delightful read for anyone who wishes to be luckier (which is probably all of us).

—**Phanish Puranam**, *Roland Berger Chaired Professor of Strategy and Organisation Design at INSEAD, France and author of* The Microstructure of Organizations *and* Corporate Strategy

This highly interesting book takes an often misunderstood concept, luck, and explains how it needs to be interpreted and more importantly, how it can be used effectively in business strategy. The examples are lively and accessible, and the theory is very useful for entrepreneurs, managers, and investors in all fields.

—**Pinar Ozcan**, *Professor of Entrepreneurship and Innovation at the University of Oxford, UK*

Fortune and chance play big roles in business and economic life in general, yet are often underestimated, as Chengwei Liu points out expertedly in his careful and engaging book. What I loved most about Liu's exposé is that he takes the notion of luck and explains how it can be managed systematically to your advantage. He shows compellingly that the best strategies are usually those that optimize the odds

—**Freek Vermeulen**, *Professor, London Business School, UK and author of* Business Exposed *and* Breaking Bad Habits

My grandmother taught me that success comes to those who work hard. To which my grandfather replied: and to those who are lucky. Ever since, I wondered about the role of luck in life. This book provides a systematic framework to understand the role luck plays in domains such as sports, financial markets, academic publishing, or firm survival. Combining a diverse set of arguments from behavioral economics, psychology, sociology and statistics, the author argues that "luck" is more than just a residual, something that we can't explain, but something that we can measure and exploit for strategic purposes.

—**Balázs Kovács**, *Professor, Yale School of Management, USA*

This world is full of successful senior executives who are smart, but realize they got lucky. And it is full of others who got lucky, but think they were smart. Read this book and decide which you are.

—**Richard D'Aveni**, *Bakala Professor of Strategy at the Tuck School of Business, Dartmouth College, USA and bestselling author of* Hypercompetition *and* The Pan-industrial Revolution

Liu's book is a fabulous treatment of luck, and is filling a much-needed gap for managers and management scholars. Every manager interested in discerning whether decision outcomes are the product of luck or skill should read it. As should every scholar or manager needing a structured treatment of luck and how it might be used strategically. His insights are paradoxical.

—**Timothy Folta**, *Thomas John and Bette Wolff Family Chair of Strategic Entrepreneurship, University of Connecticut, USA and Chair of the Strategic Management Division of the Academy of Management*

An insightful and highly entertaining tour of the counter-intuitive world of luck, skill, praise and blame, by one of its leading researchers.

—**Nick Chater**, *Professor of Behavioural Science at Warwick Business School, University of Warwick, UK and author of* The Mind is Flat

To be lucky or not to be lucky, that's a mathematical as well as a behavioural question. This book challenges the conventional wisdom of luck and shows that luck not only has five different images, but also can be measured for its impacts or used for plotting strategic moves. If you believe that luck is something that cannot be manipulated, you need to prepare to change your mind. The book of "Luck" will tell you a rather different story of chance. This book will not give you luck, but you may know how to become luckier after reading it.

—**Ruey-Lin Hsiao**, *Professor at the National Cheng-Chi University, Adjunct Professor at the National Singapore University and author of* Research without Numbers

Luck is a great but largely unacknowledged force in the world of business. Chengwei Liu is a skilled and hugely informed navigator through luck's intriguing labyrinths.

—**Stuart Crainer and Des Dearlove**, *founders of Thinkers50*

Fabulous (behavioural) science, explaining why second really is the best and how, by consistently underestimating the role luck plays in success, we undermine our own success! A much needed book that lays bare the truth about luck.

—**Helen Bagnall**, *Founder and Director, Salon London and Also Festival*

This book is a "must read" for anyone interested in social systems that produce "winners and losers"—such as business, athletics and education. It will change the way you think about what the term "luck" means—and could mean—when we think about social systems. The book tackles fundamental issues of how to use models in the social sciences and offers more nuanced approaches to luck in theory building. It also offers immediately applicable ideas about how business schools could do a better job teaching MBA students in terms of aspirations and realistic understanding of what drives outcomes. This is a highly recommended volume. Although somewhat technically demanding in parts, it is clearly written and will be invaluable for doctoral students and scholars who explore dynamics of competitive systems.

—**Anne Miner** *(Ph.D., Stanford), Professor Emerita, University of Wisconsin, Madison, USA; Winner, Scholar of the Year, Technology and Innovation Management Division, Academy of Management, 2004; Distinguished Fellow, Academy of Management; Director Emeritus, Initiative for the Study of Transformational Entrepreneurship (INSITE)*

Luck is everywhere. Sometimes, that's hard to admit, especially for managers who must make high-stakes decisions. This book will help you understand luck better, make you more comfortable with it, and maybe even help you take advantage of it.

—**Peter Stone**, *Associate Professor of Political Science, Trinity College Dublin, Ireland*

LUCK

Case studies of business and management success tend to focus on factors such as leadership, innovation, competition, and geography, but what about good fortune? This book highlights luck as a key idea for business and society.

The author provides insights from economics, sociology, political science, philosophy, and psychology to create a brief intellectual history of luck. In positioning luck as a key idea in management, the book analyzes various facets of fortune such as randomness, serendipity, and opportunity. Often overlooked given psychological bias toward meritocratic explanations, this book quantifies luck to establish the idea in a more central role in understanding variations in business performance.

In bringing the concept of luck in from the periphery, this concise book is a readable overview of management which will help students, scholars, and reflective practitioners see the subject in a new light.

Chengwei Liu (Ph.D., Cambridge) is Associate Professor of Strategy and Behavioral Science at the ESMT Berlin, Germany and the University of Warwick, UK.

Key Ideas in Business and Management
Edited by Stewart Clegg

Understanding how business affects and is affected by the wider world is a challenge made more difficult by the disaggregation between various disciplines, from operations research to corporate governance. This series features concise books that break out from disciplinary silos to facilitate understanding by analysing key ideas that shape and influence business, organizations and management.

Each book focuses on a key idea, locating it in relation to other fields, facilitating deeper understanding of its applications and meanings, and providing critical discussion of the contribution of relevant authors and thinkers. The books provide students and scholars with thought-provoking insights that aid the study and research of business and management.

Hierarchy
A Key Idea for Business and Society
John Child

Feminism
A Key Idea for Business and Society
Celia V. Harquail

Luck
A Key Idea for Business and Society
Chengwei Liu

For more information about this series, please visit: www.routledge.com/Key-Ideas-in-Business-and Management/book-series/KEYBUS

LUCK

A Key Idea for Business and Society

Chengwei Liu

Routledge
Taylor & Francis Group

LONDON AND NEW YORK

First published 2020
by Routledge
2 Park Square, Milton Park, Abingdon, Oxon OX14 4RN

and by Routledge
52 Vanderbilt Avenue, New York, NY 10017

Routledge is an imprint of the Taylor & Francis Group, an informa business

British Library Cataloguing-in-Publication Data
A catalogue record for this book is available from the British Library

Library of Congress Cataloging-in-Publication Data
A catalog record for this book has been requested

ISBN: 978-1-138-09424-6 (hbk)
ISBN: 978-1-138-09426-0 (pbk)
ISBN: 978-1-315-10614-4 (ebk)

Typeset in Bembo
by Apex CoVantage, LLC

CONTENTS

FIGURES

1

THE UNCONVENTIONAL
WISDOM OF LUCK

Consider two performances from professional sports. On the one hand, we have the New England Patriots, who won 100% of the games in Season 2007. On the other hand, we have the Chicago Bulls, who won 88% of the games in Season 1995/96. Both performances are somewhat exceptional. However, which of the two is more impressive?

If you answered the New England Patriots, you belong to the majority. Surveys distributed to 416 MBA students from 12 different cohorts at two large international universities show that 62–75% answered the New England Patriots. Only 10–15% answered the Chicago Bulls. The rest chose not to answer or argued that the question was misleading because the two sports were from different contexts: The New England Patriots are from the National Football League (NFL), while the Chicago Bulls are from the National Basketball Association (NBA).

While choosing not to answer this "misleading" question is quite sensible, prior studies suggest an alternative reason that favors the Chicago Bulls instead of the New England Patriots: The former's less extreme performance can be more impressive than the latter's perfect performance. The reason is that exceptional performances tend to occur in exceptional circumstances (Denrell and Liu 2012). A perfect performance of 100% winning percentage can be less reliable because it occurs in the NFL, with only 16 games in one season compared to the NBA's 82 games per season. Extreme values in averages are more likely to be observed with a smaller sample size. This implies that an extreme performance (e.g., season winning percentages) in the NFL can be a less reliable predictor of future performance than that in the NBA. In fact, both exceptional performances declined in the following season; however, the extent of the decline was much greater for the New England Patriots' more unreliable performance (dropped from 100% in 2007 to 69% in 2008) than the Chicago Bulls' more reliable one (dropped from 88% in 1995/96 to 84% in 1996/97).

The above example is anecdotal;[1] however, it illustrates three important aspects of the theme of this book: "the unconventional wisdom of luck." First, I will argue that top performers are likely the luckiest rather than the ablest. People often believe that top performers deserve all the reward and attention because they are the ablest (Frank 2016). Similarly, people tend to punish the least capable performers because they seem to be the least mindful or skilled. After all, conventional wisdom suggests that chance favors the prepared mind and that those who work harder tend to get luckier (Collins and Hansen 2011). Good and bad luck happens to all; however, the greatest (or the worst) performers cannot simply be (un)lucky.

I will demonstrate that such conventional wisdom of luck only makes sense for the moderate range of performances. For the most extreme performers—such as teams with exceptional performances like the New England Patriots, investors with impeccable track records, founders of billion-dollar businesses, managers involved in unprecedented disasters—luck and self-reinforcing mechanisms likely play a much greater role than the merit and effort of the persons involved.

Thus, the unconventional wisdom of luck suggests that one should search for less extreme performers, such as the second-best, as role models or investment targets. In Chapter 2, I will elaborate on the logic of the unconventional wisdom of luck through a review of five distinct interpretations of luck in the literature—luck as attribution, randomness, counterfactual, undeserved, and serendipity—and discuss their shared implication: Exceptional performances in modern societies are usually too good to be true—they likely reflect exceptional luck rather than exceptional merit.

Second, I will argue that luck can be defined, quantified, and measured. Conventional wisdom usually considers luck as the residue—unsystematic variance that cannot be meaningfully measured or analyzed (Rescher 1995). In fact, the role of luck can be quantified systematically when one connects luck to the idea of regression to the mean: Luck has a greater impact on performances when the expected future performances are more regressive (e.g., the way New England Patriots' perfect performances regressed). I will demonstrate this approach using both conceptual models and real-world data.

Thus, the unconventional wisdom of luck suggests that one can measure how the impact of luck is localized: Some performance ranges and contexts are more sensitive to luck than others. My approach also allows one to judge who is the (un)luckiest and the extent to which their successes (or failures) will persist, which has important implications for reward, learning, and competition. In Chapter 3, I will define the degree of luck using computational models and then use empirical data from sports, academia, and business to illustrate the extent to which performances are to persist (due to merit) or regress to the mean (due to luck).

Third, I will argue that one can strategize with luck. Conventional wisdom usually portrays luck as uncontrollable and that strategists should focus on the non-random factors instead of wasting time with chance (Barney 1997; Porter 1996, p. 199). I will show that there are rooms for strategizing with luck—not because there are systematic ways to get luckier than others but because the ways people are fooled by randomness are non-random and predictable.

Thus, the unconventional wisdom of luck suggests that the predictable misperception of luck can illuminate an alternative source of competitive advantage for *you*, as the more informed strategist, when your rivals over- or underestimate the value of strategic resources because they suffer from an illusion of control or are fooled by regression to the mean. In Chapter 4, I will elaborate on this contrarian approach to exploiting other people's misperceptions of luck and demonstrate by using examples from business and sports betting—spoiler alert—that you can gain a profit by short selling on the New England Patriots' perfect performances.

In summary, this book challenges the conventional wisdom of luck and introduces multiple approaches (conceptual models, empirical illustrations, case studies) to interpret, quantify, and strategize with luck. In particular, Chapter 2 provides a systematic review of the various perspectives on luck; Chapter 3 focuses on how to quantify luck using both conceptual models and empirical data. Chapter 4 explains how to gain an advantage by strategizing with luck. These three chapters are related, but with distinct approaches to unpacking luck, so each can be read independently of other chapters. Finally, in Chapter 5, I will connect these unconventional ideas of luck to how various cultures interpret luck and conclude the book by discussing how management education can reconcile the conventional and the unconventional wisdom of luck.

Note

1 I will revisit this example in Chapter 4 and show how ignorance of regression to the mean can generate an alternative source of profit.

2

HOW TO INTERPRET LUCK?[1]

Why do some people succeed more often and for longer than others? For this question—arguably central to management scholarship—one finds various explanations. Some argue that the context of a firm's operations, including industry sector and competitive dynamics, plays an important role in its performance (Porter 1980). Others argue that the resources and capabilities that a firm can control play a crucial role in explaining why some outperform others (Barney 1991; Helfat et al. 2007). There is an ongoing debate on what determines a firm's successes. A recent meta-study shows that even after adjustments for sample size and variance decomposition techniques, on average, 45% of the performance variances cannot be attributed to systematic factors, such as industry, corporate, or firm effects (Vanneste 2017). This observation joins a steady line of scholarly contributions in the management scholarship that explicitly cite luck as an explanation for performance differences (Alchian 1950; Arthur 1989; Denrell 2004; Denrell et al. 2015; Frank 2016; Hannan and Freeman 1989; Levinthal 1991; Lippman and Rumelt 1982; March and March 1977). Yet such references remain the exception rather than the rule: A review of the use of luck in leading management journals over the past five decades suggests that only 2% of articles have the word "luck" in their main text, abstract, or title (Liu and de Rond 2016), the reasons for which may not be hard to find. After all, how is one to operationalize—let alone draw practical implications from—something as fickle and haphazard as luck?

A lack of explicit reference to luck does not mean that management researchers have discounted its importance. Occasionally, they have used alternative constructs to acknowledge something quite similar. Where luck is referenced, its meaning can vary widely. For some, it is the unexplained variances that lack pragmatic value (Porter 1991). Barney (1997, p. 17) writes, what prescriptive advice can we give to managers given that the role of luck is important "that they should 'be lucky'"? For others, luck could explain performance differences because randomness in structured environments can produce systematic patterns (Denrell 2004; Denrell et al. 2015; Levinthal 1991; March and March 1977). Still, others argue that while good and bad luck can happen to anyone, some are more prepared than others (de Rond 2014), for example, by being mindful enough to rebound from bad luck or by securing a higher "return on luck" (Collins and Hansen 2011). Some even argue that other people's systematic underestimation of luck can signal profitable opportunities (Denrell et al. 2019; Denrell and Liu 2012).

The primary purpose of this chapter is to provide a systematic review of the use of luck in the management literature and in such related disciplines as economics, sociology, and psychology on which management scholars frequently draw. After defining the concept of luck, this review will identify and unpack five distinct interpretations of the role of luck: (a) luck as attribution, (b) luck as randomness, (c) luck as counterfactual, (d) luck as undeserved, and (e) luck as serendipity.

2.1 Defining luck

The New Oxford Dictionary of English (NODE) defines "luck" as "good or bad things that happen to you by chance, not because of your own efforts or abilities." Implied in this definition are three characteristics. First, luck is a psychological attribution people use to respond to observed events. In other words, people are likely to attribute an event to luck if they consider that the event happened by chance or randomly (de Rond and Thietart 2007). Second, attributing an event to luck implies that the event has a salient evaluative status, which can be either "good" or "bad." Whether luck is "good" or "bad" is beholden to the observer: It is subjective and context-dependent (Rescher 1995). Third, whether luck is "good" or "bad" or plays any role at all often depends on when one takes stock. As time passes and with the unfolding of events, one's assessment of luck can change dramatically. The same event may be interpreted differently depending on the information available, the situation in which the explanation is offered, or the motivation for providing the explanation (Runde and de Rond 2010).

To illustrate this point, imagine the unpalatable: a car crash with multiple casualties. Let us assume that an exhaustive subsequent investigation finds the crash to have been a freak accident, meaning that chance played an important role. In terms of our definition, the scenario fits the three characteristics noted above. The crash lacks obvious intentional design. Also, it produced salient outcomes that can be evaluated insofar as several people lost their lives and others their relatives. And it is also true that the crash does not necessarily need to be attributed to bad luck.

Consider that A is a person who died in the crash, B is a person who would have been involved in the crash if a call had not delayed him—hence a narrow escape—and C is a person who was not directly involved in the crash and was the unfaithful wife that A was going to divorce. Apparently, A can be considered unlucky to have died in this accident. B can be considered lucky to have avoided the crash, even if he may have initially thought himself unlucky to have been delayed.[2] C is unfortunate to have lost her husband in the crash; however, if she is now able to inherit all her late husband's property, to which she would not have been entitled after divorce, perhaps she (and her lover) may be considered lucky. An observer who has been through a painful divorce may even consider A lucky to have avoided a potentially difficult process. Perceptions of luck associated with the same crash can be interpreted differently and illustrate the third characteristic of luck attribution: Luck attribution is always subjective and can change according to the information available and with a better understanding of the motivations behind the attribution.

The definition of luck used in this book is consistent with NODE and the three characteristics of attribution mentioned above. The following analysis aims to show how the application of luck in the current management literature can broaden and enrich our understanding of how interactions between chance, context, and human interventions are relevant to management.

2.2 Luck as attribution

To treat luck as attribution is its most typical application in the management literature. According to attribution theory (Hewstone 1989; Kelley 1971; Weiner et al. 1971), people tend to attribute observed outcomes to four possible factors: skill, effort, task difficulty, and luck. Consistent with our dictionary definition, people are more likely to attribute an observed outcome to luck when the cause of the outcome is considered to be external, unstable, and uncontrollable.

Attribution biases are the focus of "luck as attribution" in the management literature. For example, when evaluating one's own performances, self-serving bias suggests that people tend to attribute their successes to skill or effort and consider failures to be bad luck (Miller and Ross 1975). Such attributions can lead to over-learning from successes and under-learning from failures, resulting in an illusion of control and overconfidence (Langer 1975). People are also notoriously incompetent in interpreting outcomes that involve randomness. For example, both the "gambler's fallacy" and the "hot-hand fallacy" suggest that people hold illusory beliefs that a random sequence entails a pattern (Ayton and Fischer 2004). Moreover, instead of seeing luck as an external, random element, people often interpret luck as a personal characteristic (Darke and Freedman 1997; Maltby et al. 2008), believing that it can be manipulated (Tsang 2004).

Attribution biases are also prevalent when evaluating other people's performances. People tend to evaluate a decision based on its realized outcome rather than the decision quality and situations at the time the decision was made (Baron and Hershey 1988). Partly as a result of the halo effect (Rosenzweig 2007), executives whose decisions resulted in success are treated as heroes and those who failed as villains even when their decisions are identical (Dillon and Tinsley 2008). Such an underestimation of the role of luck is consistent with the fundamental attribution error or people's tendency to over-attribute outcomes to dispositional factors such as skill rather than to situational factors such as luck (Gilbert and Malone 1995; Ross and Nisbett 1991). Moreover, selection bias suggests that people tend to under-sample failures and focus on survivors (Denrell 2003). This implies that people draw lessons from "lucky" survivors, even when the lesson learned can be detrimental to future performance.

To ignore regression to the mean is another common bias when evaluating observed performances. More extreme performances tend to be followed by less extreme ones because extreme performance tends to be associated with extreme luck and such luck is unlikely to persist, suggesting that future performance should regress to the mean (Harrison and March 1984). Yet people appear unconvinced by statistical accounts of performance change. Instead, they tend to generate their own causal explanations for such changes. For example, regression to the mean suggests that poor performance is likely to be followed by improvement, whereas good performance is likely to be followed by a decline. However, we tend to reward others when they perform well and punish others when they perform poorly. This can lead to superstitious learning insofar as we may wrongly conclude that being nice to others can cause decline, and being nasty to others can cause improvement (Kahneman 2011). Nevertheless, these changes in performances may only reflect regression to the mean, which requires no causal explanation. Since the effect of regression to the mean is so robust (Greve 1999; Samuels 1991; Schmittlein 1989) but also so often misunderstood (Mauboussin 2012), it will be the key concept we utilize in Chapter 3 (where we outline how to measure the impact of luck in performances empirically) and in Chapter 4 (where we outline how to profit from other people's ignorance of luck in performances).

Summary

The attribution biases mentioned above offer some reasons for people's misperceptions of luck. People are likely to underestimate the role of luck (e.g., randomness and situational factors) in observed outcomes. One possible reason for this bias is that people tend to apply cognitive shortcuts by substituting a difficult question (e.g., what is the unobserved level of skill of an executive) with an easy one (e.g., what is the observed level of performance of an executive?) (Kahneman 2011). Such substitutions can be a useful heuristic, not only because they often save time and energy, but because they could be correct (e.g., higher performers are likely to be more skilled) and thus entail ecological rationality (Todd and Gigerenzer 2012). That said, such substitutions should be avoided lest errors are costly. This suggests at least three questions to guide future research.

First, when is it desirable to apply cognitive shortcuts when evaluating performance differences? The answer to this question depends on the difference in cost between two possible errors: a false positive (e.g., mistaking luck for skill) and a false negative (e.g., mistaking skill for luck). As we have seen, attribution biases suggest that people tend to commit false positive errors when evaluating performance. This may entail important motivational functions, such as when people maintain esteem and appetite for taking a risk when engaging in self-serving biases. By contrast, a tendency to err on the side of false negatives implies inaction, which is often more costly than action in evolutionary processes (Richerson and Boyd 2005). This suggests that we may be hard-wired to make more false positive errors that, even if imprecise, are often useful. The difficulty is that cognitive shortcuts that might have once been useful for our ancestors may now lead to errors that are too costly to bear in modern societies. Think, for example, of the *Columbia* Space Shuttle disaster, which resulted from evaluating lucky near-misses as successes, or of financial crises that resulted partly from rewarding analysts' and traders' luck, or even of (dubious) entrepreneurial ventures, which have arisen from the tendency to misevaluate chance as successes. In short, mistaking luck for skill may be a useful general human attribution tendency but can lead to costly errors in today's complex situations. Future efforts can focus on specifying the conditions under which such biases can lead to undesirable outcomes before suggesting remedies.

Second, how do aspirations interact with attributions about luck? Aspirations play an important role in performance evaluations (Cyert and March 1963). People adjust aspirations based on performance feedback and interpret outcomes as successes (or failures) if current performance is above (or below) such aspiration. Given that people tend to attribute success to skill and effort and failures to luck or circumstance, they are also more likely to attribute outcomes to (bad) luck when entertaining high aspirations mainly because high expectations are more likely to be followed by perceived failures and disappointments. By contrast, low aspirations are likely followed by perceived successes and by attributions that skill and hard work caused these successes. Such asymmetrical attribution patterns can entail two processes: (a) People with lower aspirations tend to improve their skill because they believe skill matters in their successes, whereas people with high aspirations tend not to improve their skill because they believe skill does not matter in their failures; (b) over time, the aspiration levels will likely converge because the improved skill of the people who may initially have low aspirations will result in successes that boost these aspirations in the future; the under-exploited skill of those who may initially have high aspirations will result in more failures, which will subsequently decrease their aspirations. In brief, people's perceived successes and failures depend on their aspirations, and different aspirations can lead to asymmetrical luck attributions with implications for subsequent actions. These processes are just some of the many possibilities of how aspiration can interact with attribution. Since successes and failures are rarely absolute but depend instead on aspirations and social comparison, incorporating the role of aspirations in attributions about luck is likely to be promising in any future research agenda.

Third, how are we to de-bias our misperceptions of luck? It may not always be necessary to de-bias imprecise attributions that entail useful functions; however, it may be desirable to help people resist the temptation of substituting a difficult question with an easy one in cases when the error can be costly. Prior research has suggested remedies for this, for example, by leading people to believe the stakes are high or by encouraging an "outside" view (based on evidence such as statistics) instead of an "inside" view (based on intuition and gut feeling) (Kahneman and Lovallo 1993). Making people aware that they are subject to attribution biases is necessary for all these de-biasing techniques to work; however, arriving at an adequate level of understanding may be difficult in practice. People might come to understand, from first-hand experience, that using intuitive attributions often works well (Hertwig et al. 2004) and extend this technique to less familiar situations, although they may find that applying their newly acquired knowledge in different situations leads to a much less positive outcome (March 2006).

Moreover, the more uncertain the world becomes, the more people seek and rely on apparently guaranteed solutions (Gimpl and Dakin 1984). This suggests that simple de-biasing techniques are unlikely to convince people to deviate from their intuitions. In accordance with recent research on "nudging" (Thaler and Sunstein 2008), instead of "changing mindsets," it may be more effective to "change context" to direct people's decisions toward better outcomes (Liu et al. 2017). Nepotism in succession, for example, has been shown to hurt family business performances. A recent study demonstrates that nepotism may emanate from "bad luck" having been augmented in an asymmetrical process of impression formation between family and non-family members (Liu et al. 2015). This suggests that de-biasing—or changing mindsets—may not suffice in altering nepotism. Instead, changing contexts by reconfiguring social ties, is more likely to be effective in addressing this challenge. Future research should take into account how techniques of nudging (or changing decision contexts) can complement conventional approaches of de-biasing (or changing mindsets) to help people attenuate the undesirable consequences resulting from (mis)perceptions of luck. I will return to this point in Chapter 4.

2.3 Luck as randomness

The second use of luck in the management literature is to highlight the random nature of behaviors in organizations and management (Cohen et al. 1972; March and March 1977; Starbuck 1994). Even if people have intentions and make conscious (or non-random) choices based on these intentions, studies show that outcomes can still appear to be dominated by random processes. Below, I discuss four main sources of randomness in organizations.

First, organizational outcomes appear random partly because outcomes are influenced by external events over which managers have little control (Pfeffer and Salancik 1978). Corporate success is influenced by the activities of competitors, the government, and external events, such as fluctuations in exchange rates (Bertrand and Mullainathan 2001). An innovative firm may be unlucky and launch a product "on budget and on schedule" only for this to coincide with a recession; a more favorable timing might have propelled this same product and firm to success. As Bill Gates admitted, "our timing in setting up the first software company aimed at personal computers was essential to our success. . . . The timing wasn't entirely luck, but without great luck, it wouldn't have happened" (cited in Mauboussin 2012, p. 13).

A series of seminal studies on sources of variance in corporate profitability illustrates the importance of events beyond managerial control. Significantly, they found that firm or industry attributes can explain at most half of the variations in performance. The unexplained proportion of variance is larger in most studies than the proportion of variance explained by any single factor. A recent meta-study of this line of research shows that the unexplained proportion is higher than the sum of the variance accounted for by all of the other factors (Vanneste 2017). This implies that much of the variance in profitability can hardly be explained by the factors that tend to be the foci in strategy textbooks.

Second, the outcome of carefully planned behavior would appear to be random if choices were based on inaccurate forecasts or an incomplete understanding of means-ends connections. Empirical studies of forecasting accuracy show that predicting important business and political outcomes is challenging (Tetlock 2005). The average absolute percentage error (i.e., (forecast-outcome)/forecast) in forecasts of macro-economic quantities (e.g., inflation, exchange rates, unemployment) by economists and analysts is about 20% (Armstrong and Collopy 1992). Forecasts about demand and product success are even less accurate, with an average absolute percentage error of close to 50% (Fildes et al. 2009). For fast-moving consumer goods, such as movies and records, even the best methods have an absolute percentage error of 70% (Lee et al. 2003).

Forecast inaccuracy limits the extent to which theories can explain persistent firm differences. If demand changes in ways that are difficult to forecast, profitability will only be weakly persistent, even if firm capabilities or costs are highly persistent. Forecast inaccuracy also partly explains why firm growth is nearly random (Geroski 2005). Capable but unlucky firms that bet on the wrong product will not grow, while firms with weak capabilities that happen to bet on the right products will, and this explains why growth rates are almost random.

Third, the outcome of organizational decisions may appear random when events are decoupled from the intentions of those who are supposed to be in charge, and this will remain the case even in stable and predictable environments. Managers have less control over important determinants of competitive advantages, such as culture and capabilities (Hambrick and Finkelstein 1987). Managers may choose wisely among alternative strategies; however, the strategy that is implemented may be very different from their initial intent (Mintzberg and Waters 1985).

Realized outcomes may differ from intended ones because those implementing firm strategy may have different incentives, may not understand what is required, or believe they know better (Powell and Arregle 2007). Inertia is another reason why realized outcomes can differ from those intended. Change

programs to reform practices and implement new routines often fail due to inertia (Hannan and Freeman 1989). Even if organizations do manage to change, the
environment may change faster than organizations can adapt. The complicated
nature of interactions in organizations and markets can also lead to unintended
consequences and changes in one part of the organization, leading to adjustments
in other parts. Such indirect effects may render the impact of any intervention
difficult to forecast. Decision processes and conflict within organizations can
also lead to outcomes that are neither understood nor intended (Cohen et al.
1972). Finally, people in organizations make mistakes that can have significant
effects. For example, two Harvard economists dramatically exaggerated the negative impacts of a high debt ratio on GDP growth (Reinhart and Rogoff 2010).
They later acknowledged their mistake with the Excel coding they had used,
which had "averaged cells in lines 30 to 44 instead of lines 30 to 49" (Herndon
et al. 2014, p. 7), excluding five countries from the analysis. Millions of people's
lives were impacted due to austerity measures justified by this research.

Fourth, an important but often neglected source of randomness in business
is competition. Competition leads to randomness because it removes obvious
opportunities and equalizes expected returns. Samuelson (1965) provided the
first formal demonstration of how competition between skilled and rational
actors in financial markets can lead to randomly fluctuating asset prices because
of equalized returns. In efficient markets, prices reflect all available information
and only change when new information becomes available that could not have
been anticipated based on past data. Stated differently, prices should only react
to unexpected news. The implication is that price changes will be unpredictable
and uncorrelated over time, consistent with empirical evidence. Stock prices are
largely unpredictable. Empirical studies of earnings announcements also show
that stock prices mainly react to unexpected changes in earnings (Beaver 1968).

Competition also leads to randomness due to strategic uncertainty. Even in
settings without uncertainty about external events, uncertainty will exist due to
the inherent difficulty of forecasting the moves of rational competitors (Camerer
et al. 2004). Consider, for example, the following entry game: A firm can enter
three different product markets, namely A, B, or C. There is high demand for
product A (with 100 consumers), moderate demand for B (30 consumers), and
limited demand for C (10 consumers). Suppose profitability simply depends on
demand and the number of firms joining a given market: Firms in market j will
make a profit equal to demand divided by the number of firms in market j.
One hundred firms contemplate entry and make their decisions simultaneously.
Which market should they choose to join? The decision depends on what the
other firms will do; however, what they actually choose to do is likely to depend
on their forecasts of what other firms will do.

The only equilibrium in this game is a mixed strategy: The probabilities of
joining markets A, B, and C are 100/140, 30/140, and 10/140, respectively. This
equilibrium ensures that the expected profitability is the same in each market
and an important implication of such a mixed strategy is that profitability will

vary randomly between different realizations of the game, even if all players are rational and adhere to this mixed-strategy equilibrium. This simple game illustrates how competition introduces strategic uncertainty. Even if nothing uncertain exists in the specification of the game (e.g., no uncertain external events impact profitability), there is strategic uncertainty that implies that profitability will vary, seemingly by luck, over time.

Summary

Randomness is often an endogenous organizational outcome produced by intentional actors. Since random processes dominate many organizational phenomena, it is sensible to attribute their associated outcomes to luck. An interesting observation is that this perspective on luck is not tied to a particular theory in the management literature. Rather, the importance of randomness is highlighted in several different research streams, such as in decision-making, in evolutionary modeling, in studies of the distributions of firm growth rates, and in studies of diffusion, CEO effects, and competitiveness (Coad 2009; Fitza 2014; Nelson and Winter 1982; Powell 2003; Salganik et al. 2006). While these contributions are not directly connected, the recurrent theme of how randomness in a structured environment can produce systematic patterns qualifies as a "random school of thought in management" (Denrell et al. 2015). Here I discuss three directions for future research.

First, selection is an underexplored process that can increase the importance of luck in outcomes. Selection tends to amplify randomness because it reduces skill differences by removing weak competitors (Barnett 2008), thus reducing the signal-to-noise ratio. March and March (1977) argue that "almost random careers" are an expected consequence of sorting in organizations that reduce the heterogeneity in skill among managers, especially at the top. If only sufficiently skilled managers make it to the next level, the difference in skills among managers who make it to the top will be small. Unless the variability due to noise (e.g., resulting from external events or unpredictable subjective performance evaluations) is also reduced, the proportion of variance in performance due to unsystematic random variation will play an increasingly important role in selection processes. Similarly, if selection reduces the variability in firm productivity (Syverson 2011), the proportion of variance explained by productivity will decline. This implies that more extreme performances are associated with greater degrees of luck and that tougher selection criteria can lead to less qualified actors being selected (Denrell et al. 2017). Future research can also extend this line of research and develop more effective selection mechanisms that depend less on luck, particularly for high-level executives.

Second, management researchers should incorporate randomness into theory building in order to develop stronger null models when examining hypotheses (Schwab et al. 2011). Explanations relying on randomness may seem unfalsifiable: One could always claim that something was due to chance; however, how could such a statement ever be tested? By making parsimonious assumptions that there is no difference among actors, these "naïve models" usually make more rigorous and detailed predictions than other theories (Starbuck 1994). Many theories in management only make point predictions about the sign of a coefficient in a regression (e.g., we theorize that the effect of x on y is positive . . .). Theories postulating randomness at the micro-level make predictions about the distribution of outcomes, thus allowing more opportunities for the theory to be falsified. This also implies that empirical analyses that can reject a naïve model that assumes no systematic difference among actors or firms can provide more rigorous support for management theories. Students of management and organizations should take randomness more seriously, particularly when luck dominates phenomena about which managers care, such as mergers and acquisitions, persistence in performance, and innovation.

Third, given the empirical support for random variation and the wide range of phenomena that have been explained by models relying on random variation, it may be possible for randomness to go beyond "naïve models" and acquire a more prominent role in management theory (Denrell et al. 2015). In explaining an empirical regularity, a management scholar should consider explaining this regularity as a result of random variation in a structured system. In other words, it makes sense to start the search for an explanation by developing a model relying on random variation. For example, in the area of judgment and decision-making, Hilbert (2012) explored how a model of randomness (as unbiased noisy estimation) could explain several judgment regularities that had previously been attributed to cognitive biases by developing a formal model from which all regularities could be derived. Can a similar unifying formal framework be developed to explain regularities in performance persistence, career development, firm size, risk-taking, and survival? Chance models exist for each of these regularities; however, these separate models have not yet been integrated theoretically (Denrell et al. 2015). Can a formal framework be developed from which all of these regularities could be derived? Can identical assumptions about probability distributions and ideally the same parameter values be used? A unified chance model to explain various phenomena central to the field of management would seem a tantalizing prospect and well within the realm of possibility.

2.4 Luck as counterfactual

Management scholars have broadened the application of luck by including the consideration of counterfactuals (Durand and Vaara 2009; March et al. 1991). An event can be considered to be a matter of luck if it only happens in the realized world but not in most possible counterfactual worlds (Pritchard 2005). In other words, realized history is not necessarily efficient (Carroll and Harrison 1994) and can be considered as drawn from a pot of possible histories. If one could rerun the draw, how likely is it that an alternative history to that realized could be obtained? If counterfactual simulations show that the realized history is, in fact, an unlikely outlier in the distribution of possible histories, what actually happened can be considered luck.

The analysis of counterfactual histories can be problematic because the course of history is often sensitive to changes in initial conditions, and these changes can be augmented in a path-dependent process (Arthur 1989; Page 2006). For example, observed performance differences may seem to result from differences in skill rather than luck. However, if we consider the developmental process of skill, differences in skill may be due to small differences in initial conditions, for example, being in the right place at the right time. An exceptional performer may be better than any of her counterparts in realized history (i.e., what actually happened) but may not have been able to acquire those very skills in most other counterfactual histories (i.e., what could just as likely have happened). The exceptional performer may be better than others; however, his or her acquisition of superior skill can be attributed to luck or factors beyond their control (Frank 2016).

Consider an example popularized by Malcolm Gladwell. Ice hockey is the most popular professional sport in Canada (Barnsley et al. 1985). Many Canadian children aspire to become a professional hockey player, but how can this be achieved? Research has found a robust empirical regularity in the profile of Canadian professional hockey players: In every elite group of hockey players studied, at least 40% were born between January and March. This regularity seems to suggest that those born between January and March are more talented at playing hockey than the others, and the secret of becoming a professional hockey player in Canada lies in birth dates. This example is actually quite a useful illustration of how luck is amplified by path dependency. High performers from each age-group of hockey-playing Canadian children are selected and groomed for inclusion at the next level. However, there is a rule: The cutoff age for each new hockey league is the first of January. This means that those who were born in the first three months are older and likely have greater physical maturity than their peers in the same age class. They are more likely to be chosen to play more often and at higher levels where they will have better teammates, better training, and more game experience (Pierson et al. 2014). Their advantage is not so much that they are innately better at hockey but only that they are older and stronger. Nevertheless, after a few years of this selection process and the advantages arising from it, the players who were born in the first three months will likely end up being better than their peers who may have had the potential to have been as good or even better.

Chance (in this case the birth date of Canadian children) and context (selection and training in Canadian hockey leagues) are likely to play more important roles than innate merit in determining who ends up becoming a professional hockey player. Both elements of chance and context are beyond the foresight and control of Canadian children (but not their parents, of course, who have a reasonable expectation of being able to plan the child's conception). The initial slight difference in birth dates and thus physical maturity can be augmented in a path-dependent process and produce huge differences in eventual outcomes. This is occasionally referred to as the "relative age effect" (Musch and Grondin 2001). If history could be rerun with a slight difference in the initial condition (e.g., the age cutoff point being first of July, instead), it is sensible to predict that a large fraction of the current professional hockey players would have had to settle in different career paths.

The example above suggests that luck can have enduring effects on determining performance differences. The slight advantage gained due to factors beyond one's control is usually augmented in a path-dependent, rich-get-richer process (i.e., a "Matthew Effect")[3] (Merton 1968). Exceptional performances may have little to do with initial levels of skill, although they merely reflect contexts where rich-get-richer dynamics are stronger. Similar processes have been documented in a variety of research. For example, performance differences can be considered a matter of luck in the context of wealth accumulation (Levy 2003), status hierarchy (Gould 2002), technology adoption (Arthur 1989; David 1985), cultural markets (Elberse 2013; Salganik et al. 2006), business competition (Lieberman and Montgomery 1988), and even academia (Levitt and Nass 1989; Merton 1968). A shared feature of this line of research suggests that the eventual performance distribution can reflect an exaggerated or even distorted initial quality or merit distribution arising from luck (Lynn et al. 2009). Exceptional performers in these contexts should not necessarily impress us because the winners are likely to have enjoyed the early luck of the draw, and differences can be seen between alternative histories.

People's perceptions do not necessarily reflect the role of luck for at least two reasons. The first arises from the challenges involved in gaining the materials that are necessary for constructing alternative histories. Perfect counterfactual analysis is impossible if one cannot specify all of the initial conditions that could have altered the course of history. This constraint makes counterfactual analysis less practical. The second reason is due to the way people construct alternative histories in retrospect. Consistent with hindsight bias (Byrne 2005; Fischhoff 1975; Kahneman and Miller 1986), the realized history is more salient than others, making people's counterfactual imagination anchor in it and underestimate how histories could have unfolded differently. Instead of mentally simulating possible counterfactual histories, people create positive or affirming stories that emphasize how human intention and intellect trump uncertainty and difficulty (March 2010). These positive stories give their tellers and audiences a sense of identity and practical lessons for future actions, although they may not provide the best reflection of what might have been: "A good story is often less probable than a less satisfactory one" (Kahneman et al. 1982, p. 98). These human-centric stories "can be seen as possibly reflecting elements of human conceit about the role of human intention and intellect in human behaviors" (March 2010, p. 41). As a result, people often overestimate the role of skill and underestimate the role of luck in their counterfactual imaginations, mistaking luck for skill.

Summary

To regard luck in terms of counterfactuals broadens its application by considering how likely the realized history could have happened differently. By simulating the distribution of possible histories, a realized history may be attributed to luck if most alternative histories could have unfolded in very different ways. While offering a useful, normative approach of conceptualizing luck, rigorous counterfactual analysis is often difficult because one is unlikely to exhaust all initial conditions that could change the course of history. On the other hand, the way people construct counterfactual histories is often biased. We tend to focus on realized history and do not consider how things might have unfolded differently, and even when we do, the focus is very much on how changes in human interventions rather than situational factors could have undone the outcomes. Although these mental simulations can usefully maintain motivations and identity, they do not necessarily accurately reflect reality. This suggests at least three directions for future research.

First, future research can examine the role of luck by enhancing the effectiveness of counterfactual analysis. By computationally or mentally simulating the distribution of possible histories, one may be able to define the degree of luck of a realized event. For example, if a risky alternative leads to failure and bankruptcy in most imagined counterfactual scenarios, the fact that it is actually realized as a lucky success should not entail attention and rewards. However, such a counterfactual analysis is not easy because controlling all initial conditions and interactions with path dependency is difficult. Recent studies have suggested novel approaches to address this challenge (Cornelissen and Durand 2012; Durand and Vaara 2009). For example, some have suggested a "contrast explanation" approach: One should begin by maintaining all causal factors constant except the one that is of interest when developing alternative histories for an event (Tsang and Ellsaesser 2011). Another approach suggests that one should begin by relaxing key assumptions of existing explanations and developing alternative histories in a more open-ended fashion (Alvesson and Sandberg 2011) in contrast to the lab experimental fashion of a "contrast explanation" approach. These approaches all help generate plausible counterfactual histories more systematically. Management researchers could apply them when analyzing management phenomena, as has been done in fields such as political science (Tetlock and Belkin 1996) and military history (Cowley 2002), in order to refine these approaches and enhance the understanding of the role of luck in management.

Second, failing to simulate accurate alternative histories mentally can be costly. For example, a shared feature of many organizational disasters is the high number of near-misses—successful outcomes in which chance plays a role in averting failures—before actual disasters (Perrow 1984; Starbuck and Farjoun 2005; Vaughan 1997). These lucky outcomes are usually interpreted as successes, and people do not consider how the same managerial decision could have led to a disaster, boosting a false sense of security and an appetite for risk-taking. The following example from Dillon and Tinsley (Dillon and Tinsley 2008, p. 1437) illustrates this point:

> On many shuttle missions before the Columbia disaster, foam debris detached from the shuttle, but luckily never hit a highly sensitive portion of the orbiter. Lacking an obvious failure, NASA managers interpreted the many near-misses as successes and accepted the detachment of foam as an ordinary occurrence. What was originally a cause for concern no longer raised alarms; deviance became normalized.

Chance averted failure in the cases of these near-misses but did not do so with the eventual disaster. Nevertheless, NASA managers interpreted near-misses as successes and did not consider how near-misses might easily have turned into disasters. Their perceived risk of the foam-related problem was, therefore, lowered even if the statistical risk of the problem remained the same. More generally, near-misses signal the vulnerability of the underlying systems and offer opportunities for organizations to fix the problem; however, people's biased responses mean systems remain vulnerable and the potential for "normal accidents" will remain (Perrow 1984). In short, the way people mentally simulate alternative histories is problematic, particularly for near-misses in interdependent systems. This suggests an urgent need to examine how to help people construct less-biased alternative histories in order to improve their ability to evaluate risk. Future research can examine whether encouraging people to take an "outside" view (Kahneman and Lovallo 1993) or inducing people to consider "what-if" scenarios systemically could help people evaluate the outcomes that involve chance more effectively.

Third, this perspective on luck offers a new angle on an old debate about skill versus luck. Earlier studies have shown that rich-get-richer dynamics and chance elements render performance unpredictable and lead to a weak association between ability and success, implying that success is only a weak signal of skill. However, prior studies have not challenged the idea that top performers are the most skilled and worthy of reward and imitation. More recent studies have shown that the belief that top performers are the most capable is flawed because exceptional successes usually occurs in exceptional circumstances (Denrell et al. 2017; Denrell and Liu 2012). Top performers are lucky for having benefitted from rich-get-richer dynamics that boosted their initial fortune. This implies that if history was to be rerun, fortune would likely befall others. Imitating the most successful in realized history can lead to disappointment or even disasters. Even if one could imitate everything that the most successful did, one would not be able to replicate their initial fortune and path dependency.

In contrast, less extreme performances may be a more reliable indicator of skill. These "second-best performers" are likely to achieve similar levels of high, albeit not the highest, performances in most possible counterfactual histories. No rule exists for becoming the richest above a certain performance level because achieving exceptional performance usually requires doing something different or new, and there can be no recipe for such innovation. The implication is that the more extreme a performance is, the less one can learn from it because this realized outlier is more likely to indicate unreliability and could have happened differently in alternative histories. This also implies that many top performers should be dismissed, and less extreme performers (i.e., the second-best) should be rewarded and imitated.

2.5 Luck as undeserved

The fourth application of luck in the management literature centers around the praise and blame associated with the unintended consequences of managerial action. Realized outcomes are not determined solely by intentional design—uncontrollable and unpredictable factors can interfere and produce consequences that are decoupled from intention. This suggests that good intentions do not necessarily lead to desirable outcomes and vice versa. Nevertheless, laypersons tend to determine praise and blame primarily based on realized outcomes. Thus, this creates a mismatch: Well-intended actions or competent managers are blamed for failures beyond their control, while ill-intended actions or incompetent managers are rewarded for achievements that were beyond their control. Most of what falls within this category see luck as the residue of intentional design and focus on how people and organizations over- or under-reward/-punish the actors for their good or bad luck. In particular, three lines of distinct literature elaborate on how managers can receive undeserved blame or rewards.

The first line of literature relates to executive compensation and specifically to how it is that executives can receive compensation well beyond what they deserve. This is a central research topic in the literature of agency theory (Fama 1980; Jensen and Meckling 1976; Milgrom 1981) because inappropriate incentive structure can distort executives' motivation. Two common observations are that (a) executives are often paid for good luck due to factors beyond their control, such as unanticipated foreign exchange (Bertrand and Mullainathan 2001), and that (b) executives tend to be over-paid—more than their current performances can justify (Bebchuk and Fried 2009). Research has suggested several reasons for the exaggerated executive compensation. For example, top executives gain power over the board, so the board conforms to executives' self-serving request of high pay. Also, executives are aware that they can be made scapegoats when performance declines even when such decline is beyond their control (Boeker 1992). Requesting a high compensation package is as if buying insurance for situations when they can be blamed for bad luck. Overall, this research suggests that the extent of over-pay increases with executive levels, and many top executives' performances cannot justify the high compensation they receive. This can hurt firms' performances and create concerns about trust and fairness.

The second line of literature on "luck as undeserved" originates from philosophy and specifically from "moral luck" in moral philosophy (Nagel 1976;

Williamson 1981). Moral judgments should never depend on luck. After all, it is reasonable to expect people to take full responsibility for the consequences of voluntary actions and not be blamed for actions and outcomes that are beyond a person's control. Yet moral judgments often appear to be influenced by luck and circumstances.

Consider two managers facing an identical business scenario—a go/no-go case that requires a judgment call from them. They both feel that they have conducted enough analyses and are abiding by all the rules, and so both managers decide to go ahead with the plan. In one case, purely by chance, this business plan created an unanticipated, negative side effect that killed several people, while everything went well according to plan in the other case.[4] Normatively, one should not blame one manager more than the other because the difference in the consequences, however dramatic, is due to chance. However, people tend to judge otherwise—the former manager tends to be blamed and held responsible for the casualties even when they are due to bad luck.

Why do we then blame people for their bad luck? Researchers in moral psychology have proposed several explanations, all of which center around the second-order inferences one might draw from unlucky incidences. For example, the unlucky incidence that befell the first manager may indicate false beliefs held by that manager (Young et al. 2010). Both managers "felt" they had done enough analyses to justify their decision. However, perhaps the bad outcome in the first case indicates that the analyses done by the first manager were simply not rigorous enough. The first manager may have omitted some important information and wrongly evaluated the safety procedure of the plan. Therefore, the bad luck the manager experienced would not have been entirely beyond the manager's control. Another possible inference involves judging the character of the manager based on the observed outcomes (Pizarro et al. 2003). The motivation of moral judgment is ultimately about judging other people's moral character—one should avoid interacting with a person who is perceived to be immoral. The bad luck the first manager experienced may be informative about his or her character: Being reckless or imprudent, for example, means the manager deserves to be blamed (Uhlmann et al. 2015). This is also consistent with the research on the belief in luck: Lucky or unlucky outcomes are associated with perceived personal characteristics (Maltby et al. 2008). Overall, research on moral luck suggests that people's moral judgment is not neutral to luck: Laypersons as naïve moralists tie their judgment to consequences and discount the role of luck and circumstances. Nevertheless, there is an ongoing debate about the mechanisms underlying such regularities in moral judgment.

The third line of literature under this perspective on luck concerns how people evaluate executive accountability after extreme failures. Executives and operators are often blamed for large-scale failures (Perrow 1984)—be they oil spills, nuclear plant disasters, or financial crises—and expected to take responsibility and either resign or get fired. Prior studies on disaster dynamics have emphasized the role of bad luck in failures: System failures can result from exogenous factors hitting a fragile system. Systems may be so tightly coupled that even a small external shock can cascade and collapse the system due to its interactive complexity. Consider again how the *Columbia* Space Shuttle broke apart after a piece of foam insulation struck its left wing rather than the other places in previous missions (Starbuck and Farjoun 2005). System failures can also result from endogenous processes. Non-novel interruptions can cumulate to such an extent that they create additional interruptions faster than the executives in charge can fix the existing ones (Rudolph and Repenning 2002), leading to an inevitable system collapse after passing a tipping point. For example, consider how the Tenerife Air Disaster, the deadliest accident in aviation history, unfolded with several factors such as the terrorist attack, weather, and the airport capacity exacerbating the situation to the point that they set the disaster in motion and beyond the pilots' control. Overall, these studies suggest that the situational factors, such as the system characteristics and the external circumstances, are necessary to produce extreme failures. The implication is that failed executives do not deserve to take all the blame: Some of them may simply be at the wrong time and the wrong place.

Summary

This perspective on luck emphasizes a mismatch: Realized outcomes do not necessarily reflect intentions. Nevertheless, people tend to judge the quality of the actor by outcomes. This suggests that some individuals can be over-blamed for bad luck while others are over-rewarded for good luck. In particular, top executives can be over-compensated for high performances beyond their control and over-blamed for disasters that are equally beyond their control. This creates problems not only for incentive structure but also for system robustness: Unlucky executives are fired, and the system remains fragile, awaiting the next "normal accident" (Perrow 1984).

Moreover, management researchers also recognize the importance of moral luck in business. One challenge is that most empirical research on moral luck is based on people's judgment of simplified scenarios: Two similar individual actions lead to very different outcomes, and people tend to judge the individuals differently based on small modifications of the scenarios. It is not clear whether these findings are readily applicable to managerial contexts where uncontrollable forces often comprise a combination of social influences and incentive structures. Consider, for example, a case discussed by Arendt (1963) of a German soldier who served in Auschwitz. He was following orders to torture and kill prisoners as did most of his peers, and the cost of disobeying the orders might well have been his own death. To what extent should we blame him for his involvement in the Holocaust? Or consider a less extreme example: If a manager goes ahead with a mission partly because of an approaching deadline knowing that the cost of missing such a deadline is probably his or her job (Dye et al. 2014), to what extent should he or she be blamed if the plan goes wrong? These are the sorts of difficult questions about moral luck that have not been addressed systematically in management yet. This said, there are three further directions for future research.

First, when should we blame executives for failure? Normal accident theory suggests that unsuccessful executives tend to be over-blamed. However, alternative theories have suggested that the persons in charge should be blamed for extreme failures. Extreme failures can result from cascading errors that are beyond executives' control. However, the trigger of a cascade of errors is not entirely independent of the executives' skill. Clearly, poorly skilled executives can exacerbate the situation and cause the system to collapse. Tightly coupled systems can still perform reliably and be failure-free if the executives in charge are mindful enough to overcome inertia and be resilient against the unexpected before additional damages are done (Weick and Sutcliffe 2006). For example, the *Columbia* Space Shuttle disaster could have been averted had the executives at NASA paid attention to, rather than normalized, the deviances (i.e., the broken foam insulation) and interpreted previous near-misses not as successes but as a cause for concern. Overall, the studies on high-reliability organizations suggest that mindfulness, as an important dispositional factor, is crucial for complex organizations with high-risk technologies to continue performing reliably. The implication is that failures are informative about skill—the unsuccessful executives are likely to be the mindless ones who easily succumb to inertia and enable cascading errors to happen in the first place.

Taken together, this literature contributes an important consideration when evaluating the extent to which unsuccessful executives deserve to be blamed: the interaction between the scope for skill and luck. If cumulated failures do not diminish the scope for skill, this suggests that highly skilled executives are more likely to exercise their skill and stop failures from escalating. In this case, failure is informative about low skill, and the unsuccessful executives deserve to be blamed. In contrast, if the exacerbated situations diminish the scope for skill because cascading errors overwhelm managerial interventions, the eventual failure is not informative about skill. Instead, it indicates that the system is tightly coupled and sensitive to external shocks and small errors. Unsuccessful executives cannot be blamed here because, however skilled they might be, they could not have averted failure. In particular, the magnitude of the extreme failures should not be proportional to the blame the unsuccessful executives receive when small errors can cascade and override skill—the magnitude more likely illustrates the system characteristics. The interaction between skill (e.g., mindfulness and resilience) and luck (e.g., escalated situations such as cascading errors) transcends the simple scenarios discussed in the moral luck literature and should attract more attention from management researchers. I will return to this point in Chapter 3 when discussing how to quantify these interactions.

Second, recent studies suggest an interesting asymmetry in both moral judgment and performance evaluations. In moral judgment, people tend to discount the blame associated with a bad outcome but not the praise with a good outcome

(Pizarro et al. 2003). Similarly, people tend to appreciate the role of bad luck for extreme failures but not the role of good luck in exceptional performances (Denrell and Liu 2012). A second-order inference process may account for this asymmetry: Most people assume that others want to experience good luck or put themselves in a situation that would decrease exposure to bad luck. This suggests that they discount the blame associated with failure because it is against that person's "meta-desire." By contrast, people do not discount the praise associated with success because that is consistent with that person's "meta-desire" (Pizarro et al. 2003). While this account is theoretically sound, more empirical and experimental work is needed to examine the reasons for such asymmetry, which has important implications for incentive structure and executive accountability.

Third, when should we reward success? It is sensible to reward higher-achieving performers when performance is a reliable indicator of skill and effort. Otherwise, higher-achieving performers are rewarded for their good luck because their performances depend more on situational rather than dispositional factors. Nevertheless, rewarding luck is a common business practice, particularly for the corporate elite. On the one hand, the difference in skill among the corporate elites tends to be minimal (March and March 1977), implying that their successes and failures more likely result from situational enablers or constraints.

On the other hand, people pursue a romanticized perspective on these successful stars (Khurana 2002; Meindl et al. 1985), even when star performances probably emanate from uncontrollable factors. In fact, the perceived top performers can be expected to be less skilled than their lower-performing counterparts when extreme performances indicate unreliability, such as excessive risk-taking or cheating. This implies a large discrepancy between people's romanticized perspectives on how corporate elites are responsible for firms' destiny and the reality of how luck dominates the performances beyond a certain level.

Moreover, the exaggerated high compensation of top executives creates problems for redistributive justice and endangers the stability of societies. In particular, it hurts the belief in a just world. Belief in a just world is closely related to perceptions of the extent to which outcomes should be attributed to luck (Alesina et al. 2001). It is often an illusion to believe that the world is just. To work hard, for example, does not guarantee the payoff one deserves when outcomes are mostly determined by social connections and inherited wealth (Piketty 2014). Such an illusion often entails desirable outcomes because of a self-fulfilling prophecy: Those who believe luck matters less will be motivated to work harder (Benabou and Tirole 2006; Gromet et al. 2015). Research shows that belief in a just world is a prevalent illusion (with notable differences among countries) and can explain why GDP growth is higher in the United States (with higher underestimation of luck) than in many European countries (with lower underestimation of luck). However, such misperceptions can backfire: Alesina et al. (2001) have also shown that underestimating luck has led to less social spending in the United States. If the majority believes that luck matters less and one should be responsible for one's own fate, social spending on medical care, for example, is likely to be lower, potentially decreasing social mobility and strengthening social inequality. This, in turn, can lead to social instability because beyond a certain threshold of social inequality, more people will come to realize that the world is less just than they believed it to be. The exaggerated payments to the executives and bankers, particularly after the financial crises, strengthen this impression manifested in demonstrations such as "Occupy Wall Street." Some rational accounts may explain why high executive compensation is useful; however, executives should also consider the consequences of their high compensation packages for society, lest they should decide to react to such perceived injustice more radically. Overall, this discussion suggests that rewards for high-ranking corporate executives should be proportionally less because luck plays a more crucial role in performance at higher levels in corporations. Otherwise, top executives' high compensation is not only unjustifiable but undermines the belief in a just world and increases instability in societies.

2.6 Luck as serendipity

The fifth usage of luck in the management literature emphasizes why some people and firms are luckier than others, or how "chance favors the prepared mind," as Louis Pasteur put it. Good and bad luck befall to all, but only some can maximize the return on luck. The focus is not on chance or luck per se but on individuals' or firms' traits that make them able to see what others do not see—a form of "serendipity." Before elaborating on the role of serendipity in a management context, I introduce its origin, which is a closer correlate of creativity and often associated with scientific breakthroughs and lucky industrial discoveries, such as Velcro, X-rays, aspirin, Post-it Notes, the HP Inkjet printer, and Scotchgard.

The origin of serendipity

Serendipity has its etymological origins in a 16th-century tale recounted in a letter sent by Horace Walpole to a distant cousin on 28 January 1754. In it, three princes of Serendip (present-day Sri Lanka) were sent by their father to fend for themselves to gain practical knowledge of the world when they came across a camel owner who was distraught for having lost his precious asset. He inquired as to the whereabouts of his camel. While the princes had not seen the camel, they were able to render an accurate description of it: It was lame, blind in one eye, lacked a tooth, was carrying butter on one side and honey on the other, and was being ridden by a pregnant woman. Their description was accurate enough to raise the camel owner's suspicion. He took them captive and handed them over to the emperor. Upon interrogation, it became clear that the description of the camel had been deduced from observation alone. They explained that they thought the camel was blind in the right eye because the grass had been cropped only on the left side of the road. They inferred that it was missing a tooth from the bits of chewed grass scattered across the road. Its footprints seemed to suggest that the animal was lame and dragging one foot. Also, finding ants on one side of the road and flies on the other, they concluded that the camel must have been carrying butter on the ants' side and honey on the flies' side. Finally, as for the presence of a pregnant woman, a combination of carnal desires on the part of the princes and imprints of hands on the ground sufficed to bring about this conclusion (Merton and Barber 2006).

Walpole's tale is instructive because the princes relied on creativity in recombining events (that came about by chance or happenstance) and in exercising practical judgment to deduce the "correct pairs" of events to generate a surprisingly effective (and, as it happens, entirely accurate) plot. In contrast to other perspectives on luck, serendipity points toward a distinct capability, namely that of recombining any number of observations to deduce "matching pairs" or sets of observations that appear to be meaningfully related. Serendipity is the "prepared mind" in Louis Pasteur's oft-cited quip, which enables some organizations and the individuals inside them to increase the occurrence likelihood of unexpected but meaningful discoveries. This may be what Porter (1991, p. 110) had in mind when suggesting that "there are often reasons why firms are 'lucky.'"

Serendipity in the context of discoveries and innovation

A closer examination of serendipity also suggests a typology (de Rond 2014). A first distinction is between "true" and "pseudo" serendipity, where one seeks A but finds B, and where B is ultimately more highly valued. When it came to the Nobel Prize-winning discoveries of PCR and DNA, Mullis, Francis, and Crick respectively found what they were looking for, although by way of chance. In each case, the objective remained unchanged; however, the route toward achieving this objective proved unusual and surprising.

> Crick and Watson's discovery of the "double helix" structure of DNA was marked by various unplanned events, such as Watson's loosely related work on TMV (corroborating their suspicions of a helical structure), and exchanges with Griffith and Donohue (in directing them toward the specific, but unorthodox, pairing of bases). Yet they always knew that they were after the structure of DNA, believing it to contain the secret of life. Thus, DNA illustrates pseudo-serendipity, insofar as chance events enabled the unraveling of the molecule, yet these events never caused them to deviate from this original target.
>
> *(de Rond 2014, p. 10)*

In pseudo serendipity, A is sought, and A is found but via a route quite different from that originally envisioned. In contrast, in the discoveries of sildenafil citrate (the key ingredient in Viagra) and penicillin, scientists discovered something other than what they had been seeking.

Both Fleming and Pfizer's scientists applied creativity and practical judgment in matching observations of unforeseen events with findings reported by others, and in selecting which of these combinations might be fruitful. They rightly interpreted coincidences as meaningful in the context of the knowledge available to them at the time. However, the particle from the mycology labs wafting through Alexander Fleming's open window to contaminate a bacterial culture is a random variation, as were the unusual changes in temperature. By contrast, the unanticipated side effects of sildenafil citrate surfaced in part as a result of research design; after all, toxicity trials tend to use men between the ages of 18 and 30, as did Pfizer's clinical trials.

(de Rond 2014, p. 10)

One can make a further distinction between chance as the unintended consequence of research design and chance as pure random variation. Thus, in discovering sildenafil citrate and PCR, opportunities arose as a direct consequence of the way the study had been designed: The unintended side effects of sildenafil citrate became apparent precisely because Phase 1 clinical trials used healthy male volunteers. Likewise, Mullis' discovery of PCR relied entirely on his recombination of the existing technologies. By contrast, penicillin and DNA benefitted from random chance occurrences: The spore in Fleming's dish had most likely wafted in from the mycology labs located one floor down, and Crick was fortunate to share his office with a crystallographer, who pointed out the flaws in his original "textbook-correct" model.

Serendipity in the context of management

In the context of management, we can conceptualize how chance interacts with the individual capability to coproduce serendipity in four different ways (Austin 1978). The first conceptualization holds that luck cannot be attributed to the beneficiary in any meaningful way. This application is a baseline case of luck as serendipity and is consistent with the application of luck by Jay Barney (1986). A firm's performance is determined by the values created by the strategic factors the firm owns. Superior performance is likely to be founded on the firm's superior foresight about the value of its strategic factors and from acquiring these factors for less than they are worth. Otherwise, there should be no abnormal returns—any superior performance should be attributed to good luck because profitability is ultimately traced to unexpected price changes. If strategic factors are priced correctly, based on all of the available information, price changes only occur when new, unexpected information becomes available. Therefore, this is, in fact, the baseline case *without* serendipity: Gains should be attributed to pure luck or windfall that is independent of the person.

The second variation of luck as serendipity is about how luck favors those in motion—people who are willing to venture new ways to make progress. While good luck may befall the lazy and inert, favorable outcomes are more likely to be the result of hard work joined by chance events or "practice and you get luckier" (Burgelman 2003). As Charles Kettering, the former head of research at General Motors, put it, "keep on going, and the chances are you will stumble on something, perhaps when you are least expecting it. I have never heard of anyone stumbling on something sitting there" (as quoted in Austin 1978, p. 15). Moreover, the chance of success may be low and unforeseeable. However, to continue trying will exclude the alternatives that would have led to failure, enhancing the chance of success over time. The implication is that experimentation matters, and benefits can arise from exposing oneself to situations that increase the chance of realizing favorable outcomes.

The third variation of luck as serendipity is about how luck favors those who look inward. Sometimes people or firms can pre-adapt: They happen to be endowed with strategic factors that can be recombined into a valuable, idiosyncratic strategic advantage (Cattani 2005). The holdings of these valuable strategic factors often result from unintended consequences. For example, Cattani (2005) uses the case of Corning to illustrate how an unanticipated use of fiber optics technology enabled Corning to become one of the leaders in long-distance communications. Alternatively, some idiosyncratic strategic factors can result from people's opportunistic behaviors when dealing with ambiguity and resource uncertainty. This implies that sustainable superior performances are more likely to result from an accurate understanding of firm-specific resources, even when these resources have been acquired by accident or opportunism (Cohen and Levinthal 1990). By extending these unique resources, firms are more likely to gain competitive advantages, which cannot be easily imitated by competitors.

Consider the case of Bill Gates, the founder of the software giant Microsoft (as quoted in Gladwell 2008, p. 55):

> If there were fifty [teenagers who had the kind of experience I had] in the world, I'd be stunned . . . all those [opportunities] came together. I had a better exposure to software development at a young age than I think anyone did in that period of time, and all because of an incredibly lucky series of events.

This series of lucky incidents to which Gates referred began with his wealthy family sending him to a private school with computers (rare equipment in the 1970s), which allowed him to develop his hobby of programming and to develop a unique competence relative to his cohort and competitors. After gaining superior competence, his mother's connection to IBM's then-president facilitated a contract with Gates' startup. Bill Gates augmented all of these developments by deciding to decline the most apparently sensible alternative of attending Harvard to be able to start his own company, all enabled by the series of lucky events he enjoyed. The success of Microsoft may seem lucky to many (including Gates himself) because the company would not have been so successful with slight changes in any of the conditions mentioned above. This application of luck as serendipity focuses on the role of human intervention, instead: The fact that Gates understood the value of his unique capabilities and decided to start his own business instead of going to Harvard is crucial to the establishment of the sustainable superior performances of Microsoft. Stated differently, temporary competitive advantage is possible by looking forward (i.e., forecasting the trends), looking backward (i.e., drawing lessons from histories), working hard, or just being lucky. However, sustainable competitive advantage is only possible through looking inward, that is by creating isolating mechanisms through individualized resources and capabilities that cannot be easily replicated by competitors.

The fourth variation of luck as serendipity concerns how luck favors those who are alert and flexible. Low-hanging fruits will be exploited quickly as the efficient market hypothesis suggests; however, other less obvious opportunities are likely to be left unexploited whenever the market is not perfectly efficient. Favorable chance may happen to anyone, but only those who pay attention to weak signals and are capable of recognizing and responding quickly can grasp opportunities (Denrell et al. 2003). The ability to see what others do not is the key to this application of luck, and it is this variation that most closely reflects serendipity's etymological origins. For example, the executives of Honda managed to link information that seemed to distract them from their original goal of promoting heavyweight motorcycles in the United States and concluded that lightweight motorcycles were *the* model to introduce in the US market, instead. This serendipity led to the extraordinary success in the United States of its "Supercub" in the late 1950s (Mintzberg 1996). The implication is that looking outward may be useful in addition to looking inward. Opportunities may exist even for those who do not yet possess any valuable resources (e.g., entrepreneurs) but can make meaningful combinations of seemingly irrelevant factors that were omitted by others.

Summary

The application of luck as serendipity recognizes the importance of luck in innovation and management but emphasizes that certain characteristics help some recognize chance opportunities and seize them where others do not. This perspective on luck is consistent with a primary purpose of management: to rein in randomness and gain more control over outcomes. It is perhaps not surprising that many management researchers do not use the term "luck" in their writing. Even when they do, the focus is not on luck per se but on what managers should do to get lucky. This perspective on luck also entails three directions for future explorations.

First, opportunities may exist when social dynamics discourage others from exploiting atypical opportunities—a behavioral source of market inefficiency. Prior studies have suggested that people feel more comfortable in conforming to the majority, which aligns with the idea that the majority is very often wise, so following the crowd is sensible. However, the majority can be wrong. For example, in his book *Moneyball* (2003), Michael Lewis documents how a stereotype of what good players should look like biased scouts and coaches in Major League Baseball. Opportunities, thus, existed for less resourceful teams who applied different approaches (e.g., statistical analysis) to find undervalued players who could contribute more than what was immediately suggested by traditional interpretations. Around the turn of the millennium, the Oakland A's managed to pay less for players than their eventual contribution would suggest they were worth and then resell their best-performing players (particularly closing pitchers) toward the peak of their output. They benefitted from this trading strategy because (a) they were better able to recognize the value of their players when buying them and (b) other teams paid more for these players than they might be worth when selling them, indicating how extreme performances are more likely to regress to the mean in future seasons. Such a strategy led to a higher ratio of win rates relative to salary costs than other teams and suggested that opportunities might exist but are left unexploited because they seem atypical to many due to norms, biases, peer pressure, or misperceptions of luck (e.g., ignoring regression to the mean). Recent studies have also explored such alternative sources of strategic opportunity that can result from misperceptions of luck strengthened by social dynamics (Denrell et al. 2019). I will return to this point in Chapter 4.

Second, who can grasp the atypical opportunities when others are bounded by norms or peer pressure? One possibility is that luck may favor those who are less sensitive to what others think. For example, extreme failures may indicate that the system is tightly coupled and sensitive to external shock rather than that the executives lack skill. The implication is that unsuccessful executives should not necessarily get fired because they may just be in the wrong place at the wrong time. However, many executives who experience extreme failures are fired and treated as scapegoats. Opportunities may exist for those who dare to hire unsuccessful executives because they can be hired for less than they are worth.

Nevertheless, companies who are sensitive to what stakeholders think are unlikely to hire executives associated with failures, even when they understand that the executives are skilled but unlucky, often because there is no certainty that stakeholders will be able to make this inference. More generally, opportunities exist for those who can afford to implement a contrarian strategy. By acting on accurate inferences and against the crowd, prizes can be more substantial due to less competition. In this sense, fortune may favor the insensitive—those who can afford to implement a contrarian strategy and act on atypical inferences, such as dismissing the most successful and hiring the least successful.

Third, understanding how contextual factors enable serendipitous combinations deserves more research. Applications of luck as serendipity mostly emphasize how actors manage to see what others do not see. Other studies emphasize that such serendipity should be attributed less to the actors and more to the network structure in which the actors are embedded. For example, using the analogy of solving a puzzle, Simonton (2004) suggests that most important scientific discoveries should not be attributed to a single scientist at a particular time but to other scientists who discovered the pieces necessary to solve the puzzle and to the network that enabled the recognized scientist, who eventually accessed all of the pieces that were relevant to solving the puzzle. Some studies in management and sociology also suggest the importance of network structures in enabling innovation and its diffusion (Small 2009). More generally, detailed contextual analyses of serendipitous outcomes tend to undermine the role of the "stars" involved and, instead, suggest how "exaptation" plays more important roles in enabling the outcomes (Andriani and Cattani 2016). This line of research, thus, undermines the role of actors and emphasizes the role of situational factors, such as networks, in serendipitous discoveries. Future research can extend this line of research and specify the conditions under which actors are more important than contexts for innovation.

2.7 Summary: luck is in the eye of the beholder

We discussed five distinct perspectives on luck, each of which is tied to a particular strand of literature. In addition to summarizing these strands of literature, I outlined several directions for future research. These ideas may collectively form a research agenda to help us further understand the role of luck in management.

This review should have made it clear that management researchers typically entertain quite different understandings of how luck interacts with context and human intervention. These differences reflect the distinct focuses of the subfields in management. First, luck as serendipity is mostly studied by researchers in subfields such as strategy and entrepreneurship. Their disciplinary background is often economics, which tends to focus on choice as the product of calculation and reasoning applied to a predicament. Thus, serendipity emphasizes how luck can be tamed through actors' will. An attribution-based approach (luck as attribution and undeserved) is utilized by researchers in subfields such as organizational behavior and judgment and decision-making. Their disciplinary background is often psychology, which focuses on how perceptions happen and influence behaviors. This perspective on luck as attributions emphasizes the cause and consequences of the misperceptions of luck.

Finally, the applications of luck as randomness or counterfactuals are mostly used by researchers in subfields such as organization theory and population ecology in the disciplinary background of sociology, which focuses on how choices are constrained by context. Thus, these two perspectives on luck as randomness and counterfactuals emphasize how observed outcomes are mostly determined by luck.

Overall, these perspectives on luck reflect varying assumptions about actors' degrees of freedom in outcomes: from a high degree (luck as serendipity) to a moderate degree (luck as attribution or undeserved) and a low degree (luck as randomness or counterfactual). One perspective on luck does not necessarily represent reality more accurately than the other. Instead, these diversified understandings of luck are desirable for an interdisciplinary field such as management. Nevertheless, this does beg the question: Which perspective is more applicable to a given context? When should we assume that the role of luck overwhelms merit? Can we quantify the impact of luck? I will outline some approaches to addressing these important questions in the next chapter.

Notes

1 This chapter is adapted from my 2016 paper published in *Academy of Management Annals*, co-authored with Mark de Rond at the University of Cambridge.
2 A related example is from the unfortunate crash of Ethiopian Airlines Flight ET302. Among the passengers was Antonis Mavropoulos, who got to the departure gate two minutes after it had closed due to the delay of his connecting flight, thus escaping the deadly crash that killed all 157 passengers on board. In an interview, Mr. Mavropoulos admitted that he was frustrated when he was denied boarding but then felt extremely lucky as well as a moral obligation to the 157 dead passengers to find out why the Ethiopian Airlines plane crashed.
3 Robert Merton (1968) coined this term from the Gospel of Matthew: "For to all those who have, more will be given, and they will have an abundance; but from those who have nothing, even what they have will be taken away" (Matthew 25:29, New Revised Standard Version).
4 This example is adapted from a now-classic example that Nagel (1976) developed. One of two law-abiding drivers experienced an unexpected and uncontrollable event. A young girl ran in front of the car, and this driver hit and killed the girl, whereas the other driver arrived at the destination uneventfully. Philosophers ask, "Should we blame the former driver more than the latter one?" My adapted example happens in a typical management context; however, the essence is identical to the one developed by Nagel.

3

HOW TO QUANTIFY LUCK?

Quantifying luck has a long intellectual history. Science involves activities that help humans understand the systematic structure and behavior of the natural and social world through observations and experiments. To understand the systematic factors, scientists need to separate them from the unsystematic factors (e.g., randomness, coincidence, or noise) when evaluating the observations. For instance, to what extent does a change in global temperature over time signal a systematic trend instead of random fluctuations? To what extent does an increase in test scores signal students' improvement instead of pure chance? To what extent does an impeccable investment track record signal superior foresight instead of someone getting lucky in a row? To what extent does a successful billionaire signal superior entrepreneurial capability instead of being at the right place and right time?

The answers to the above questions have important implications because they determine how we interpret and respond to what we observe. For example, if citizens think that global temperature increases as a matter of random fluctuations instead of a trend, policies that enforce a reduction in CO_2 emission will not gain support. If teachers interpret students' improved scores as enhanced skill and effort, additional rewards and resources are likely to be allocated to these students. If the majority believes that exceptional success and wealth are primarily brought about by merit instead of luck, policies that enforce a higher tax on the rich will not receive favorable support.

A challenge is that humans are not good at separating noise from signal. If left to our own devices, we tend to be fooled by randomness in various ways, as discussed in Chapter 2. This suggests that humans should not trust own intuition when judging outcomes that involve randomness and luck. More systematic approaches are needed to help humans distinguish the influence of unsystematic factors to avoid mistaking noise for signals. To this end, scientists and statisticians have introduced various ways to quantify the unsystematic factors (i.e., luck).

The purpose of this chapter is to introduce both the conventional and the novel approaches to quantifying luck. I categorize these approaches into three types: the weak, the semi-strong, and the strong versions of quantifying luck. The conventional ways center around building naïve hypotheses (weak version) or naïve models (semi-strong version) where unsystematic factors are assumed to be the key contributory factors to the phenomenon under study. If the observations deviate sufficiently from the predictions of the naïve hypotheses/models, one should then conclude that the systematic factors instead of luck are likely the better explanation for the phenomenon.

I will also introduce and demonstrate a novel approach—the strong version of quantifying luck. This approach builds on the idea of regression to the mean and enables us to measure how sensitive performances are to unsystematic factors in a particular context. It also produces a baseline for predicting the extent to which observed performances will persist or change. I will elaborate on how this approach helps us judge merit (i.e., who has superior skill instead of being lucky), thus deserving more reward and attention. This novel approach is illustrated using data from various contexts (such as the lottery, academia, professional sports, and business) to show how one can quantify the role of luck when evaluating successes and failures.

3.1 The weak version: luck as a straw man in hypothesis testing

Consider a game run with 40 students in a class. The rules are as follows: All students as players stand up at the beginning of the game. The instructor tosses a coin without showing the result to anyone. The players raise their hands if they think the result is heads; they do nothing if they think the result is tails. The instructor then displays and announces the result of the toss (i.e., heads or tails). The players who guessed it right will maintain their position, and the rest will sit down. This cycle repeats until there remains only one survivor who has guessed all the results correctly in a row.

This is the exercise I used at the beginning of my lecture on the role of luck in management. I ran this exercise for more than 50 times in various classes. In a class with about 40 students, the winner usually emerges in the fifth or sixth round.[1] I will then ask the winner about his or her strategy of guessing the coin-tossing results correctly six times in a row.

Over the years, I have received various responses from the winners. The majority of the winners simply said they won because of pure luck. After all, there is no reason to believe that the coin was unfair or someone in the room (including the instructor) had a special skill in controlling or forecasting the results. Interestingly, a few winners insisted that there was a genuine winning strategy. To win, they consciously delayed their guesses/actions until they could identify the distribution of the guesses in the room before joining the minority. This strategy does enhance the expected chance of becoming the last one standing due to reduced competition in the subsequent rounds if the minority turns out to be correct. Then I asked if he or she could replicate this win if we repeated the game. They then conceded because they could immediately see that in the most counterfactual worlds, they would not have won even when their strategy was not invalid. The outcomes are almost entirely determined by sheer luck, and this overwhelms the scope of exercising a strategy.

The setup of this game resembles that of the stock market and innovation forecasting (Barney 1997; Denrell and Fang 2010). Many fund managers or entrepreneurs brag about their winning track records, for example, beating the market ten years in a row or forecasting the next big things repeatedly. Should you be impressed by such an impeccable record?

The answer is: It depends. That is, it depends on what is the baseline probability of obtaining an impeccable record by luck. To evaluate whether a track record like beating the market ten years in a row is impressive, you need to compare it against a suitable benchmark (e.g., how many mutual fund managers should we expect to beat the market ten years in a row?). Strong evidence suggests that stock prices are somewhat random in that their rises and falls cannot be predicted systematically (Fama and French 2010; Samuelson 1965). When the market is relatively stable, the prices should incorporate all the relevant information, suggesting that the market is pretty efficient and any moves in prices should be almost random. When the market is relatively turbulent, the prices can fluctuate dramatically mixed with unexpected news and crowds' overreactions (De Bondt and Thaler 1985). Both suggest that the outcome of predicting the stock prices is not very different from tossing a coin: Roughly half of the time you may get it right and the other half wrong.

Even when the factors that determine successes and failures are a matter of pure luck, we should expect a few winners to obtain an exceptional track record when numerous investors make their guesses over time. In fact, the probability of observing a fund manager beating the market ten years in a row approaches one, when one realizes that there are tens of thousands of mutual funds operating around the globe. It would be more surprising if we did not find any fund managers obtaining such a record.

Let us formalize this thinking process based on the classroom exercise example. The question is the extent to which you should be surprised by the fact that a winner was guessing the outcomes correctly six times in a row and beating the other 39 players. Being surprised likely indicates some systematic factors centering around this winner (e.g., superior foresight or skill). Being unsurprised suggests that the outcome is entirely expected by the game setup, and the winner is likely the luck of the draw.

To examine this question, we need to compare the observation against a baseline prediction. To generate this baseline prediction, we need to make assumptions about the players' skill distribution. We first assume no skill difference in the room (i.e., all the 40 players make random guesses: 50% of the time they will say heads, or they will say tails otherwise. If we also assume the coin is fair and the instructor has no way of influencing the outcome systematically, half of the players will expectedly guess the correct answer in each round while the other half will fail. Given these assumptions, what is the expected number of winners after six rounds (i.e., the most common result I obtained in a class with 40 students)?

Figure 3.1 shows the distribution of possible outcomes and their corresponding likelihood based on one million simulations. Each simulation resembles creating a virtual classroom with 40 students playing this game for six rounds. During each round, each player has a 50% chance of guessing heads and the other 50% guessing tails, although their actual guessing in each round is stochastic. The outcome of each round (heads or tails) will be randomly chosen. Those who get it right will continue the game, and the rest will have to quit. After six rounds, the model will produce the actual number of surviving contestants. I will then repeat the simulations in identical conditions for one million times: It is as if I create one million identical classroom exercises. Each will end up with several contestants after six rounds. Figure 3.1 uses a histogram to display the distribution of the number of contestants among all these simulations.

As Figure 3.1 shows, the most likely outcome (45% chance) is that no one out of the 40 players can guess the answer correctly six rounds in a row.[2] This is not surprising when one considers the expected number of the winners: 0.5 (the chance of winning during each round) to the power of six (six rounds) times 40 (the number of players), which equals 0.625.

The next most likely outcome is as follows: There is a 35% chance of observing one winner guessing the correct answer six rounds in a row. This suggests that observing one winner, when assuming that everyone in the room is equally unskilled, is quite a likely outcome to be observed in reality. In fact, there is a 14% chance of observing two winners or a 55% chance of observing at least one

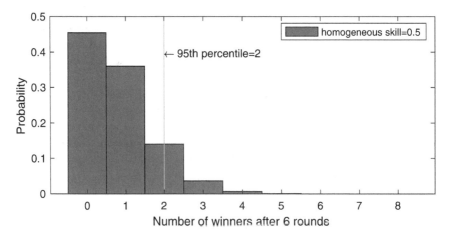

FIGURE 3.1 The simulated distribution of the number of winners of a coin-tossing game. All 40 players are assumed to have no skill in forecasting the outcomes of the tosses

winner. Given this simulation result, we should not be overly impressed by the fact that a winner was getting it right six rounds in a row because it is what one should expect from how luck operates in this game.

If you do not find the above logic and thinking process weird, you already understood the principle of one of the most important techniques of quantifying luck in statistics: hypothesis testing.[3] The first task of a hypothesis-testing process is to develop a null hypothesis (i.e., what would have happened if the outcome had been influenced purely by luck, such as sampling error or stochastic processes). In our exercise, the null hypothesis is what the outcome will look like when assuming no difference in skill, and the luck of the draw entirely determines the outcome. The source of luck in this exercise is made salient (i.e., guessing the outcome of coin tosses). In many hypothesis-testing processes, the source of luck is assumed to be sampling error; that is, there is a true underlying process or value to be estimated. However, each estimation is a combination of the true value and some noise. The idea of hypothesis testing is to assume that these errors follow a certain type of distribution, such as normal distribution. Then one compares the actual observation against the assumed error or "luck" distribution. If the observed value is so extreme that it is unlikely to be produced simply due to luck or sampling error, then one rejects the null hypothesis and concludes that there is likely a systematic difference or process underlying the observations.

An important question in the hypothesis-testing framework is as follows: How extreme is "too extreme" for rejecting a null hypothesis? The answer is to assign a "significance level." The researchers predetermine a threshold, say, a 5% significance level, which means the researcher allows a 5% chance of falsely rejecting the null hypothesis. In our exercise, we can simulate the 95th percentile value of the number of contestants after six rounds, which equals 2, as shown in Figure 3.1. This means that even if the outcome is entirely determined by the luck of the draw, there is still a 5% chance that we will observe two or more contestants after six rounds. That said, given the 5% significance level, the observation of two contestants is extreme enough to reject the null hypothesis that everyone is equally unskilled. The 5% significance level implies that researchers consider this as an acceptable risk. For more risk-averse evaluators, one can reduce the significance level, say, to 1%. Then the threshold becomes 3: One should reject the null hypothesis only when observing more than three surviving contestants after six rounds.

Many scholars have highlighted the limitations of conventional hypothesis testing (Schwab et al. 2011). For example, conventional testing is against a point estimate (e.g., critical values based on the 95th percentile). The critical values also allow one to compute the *p*-value: the probability of obtaining the observation given that the null hypothesis is correct. If this *p*-value is small enough (e.g., < 5%), then one rejects the null hypothesis and concludes that the result is unlikely to result from luck. However, testing against only a point estimate misses the opportunities of a more rigorous test. As Figure 3.1 demonstrates, one can actually test the observation against the shape of the whole distribution for all possible outcomes. The other criticism is that the null hypothesis constructed is usually too naïve. For example, assuming that people have the same skill in the class exercise may be sensible; however, in other situations, people should differ in their skill, which can imply very different critical values and conclusions. Conventional hypothesis testing does not lend itself to testing against these highly sophisticated null hypotheses, making it too naïve a straw man to be rejected (Schwab et al. 2011).

Figure 3.2 demonstrates how these two limitations can be overcome, based again on the classroom exercise example. One can assume that players have different skills. One just needs to assume varying shapes for such skill differences. For example, players can have very different skills where extremely high and low skills are both present (i.e., a uniform distribution). Or people can be different; however, most of them have no skill (i.e., a bell-shaped distribution with a mean value centering around 0.5). As Figure 3.2 shows, different assumptions can produce very different outcome shapes and critical values. A researcher can test the distribution of observations against these simulated outcome distributions to determine the extent to which observed outcome is a matter of luck.

In conclusion, there is a long tradition of quantifying luck in statistics and science more generally. Whenever one uses the hypothesis-testing approach to examine the extent to which observations entail systematic patterns, one has to quantify luck by building a baseline model or null hypothesis. The challenge is that the null hypothesis is usually too naïve to be a valid baseline. If the observation can reject a stronger null hypothesis than a naïve straw man, one can have more confidence in the research conclusion. Given humans' natural tendency for mistaking noise for signal, a straw man hypothesis increases the chance of mistaking luck for skill.

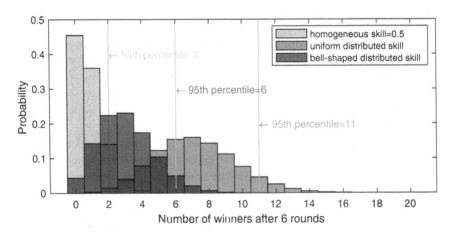

FIGURE 3.2 The simulated distribution of the number of winners of a coin-tossing game. The skill of 40 players are assumed to follow three different distributions: a homogeneous skill, a uniformly distributed skill, or a bell-shaped distributed skill

Nevertheless, null finding—the results are simply a matter of luck—looks dull to human beings. Many researchers want to show that their alternative hypothesis is correct; that is, the winner has superior foresight or skill, or exceptional performers beat or make their own luck. It is easy to set up a naïve, null hypothesis to be rejected to give the impression that the conclusion is supported by a rigorous, scientific process (Denrell et al. 2015; Schwab et al. 2011). However, quantifying luck in a naïve fashion is to allow more opportunities to be fooled by randomness.

3.2 The semi-strong version: luck as an alternative explanation for empirical regularities

A challenge of the weak version of quantifying luck is that "the theory of luck" in many hypothesis-testing frameworks is too naïve. The null hypotheses are rejected too often as a straw man and fail to produce strong support for the conclusions drawn.

One possible solution is to dispose of the straw man and develop a more sophisticated naïve model. This requires a reverse engineering approach—starting with the data and asking if this empirical regularity can be explained/reproduced by a combination of randomness and certain theoretical mechanisms (Denrell et al. 2015).

This approach helps to achieve two goals. First, if successful, it provides an alternative explanation for the empirical regularities. If this model—which assumes only chance and certain theoretical mechanisms—can reproduce the empirical regularities, it can be considered a better explanation in the spirit of Occam's razor—other things being equal, simpler explanations should be favored. Second, a good naïve model also predicts the entire distribution instead of a point prediction. One can compare the entire empirical distribution against the distributions produced by the naïve model to determine model fitness. If the distributions are different enough, then they suggest that the naïve model and its predictions are insufficient to explain the results. The logic is identical to conventional hypothesis testing, although this approach provides a stronger, context-dependent baseline for empirical examinations and are endorsed by scholars in many fields (for review, see Denrell et al. 2015).

Let us consider an example from population ecology. Based on multiple empirical findings, a stylized fact is that the probability of failure usually has a unimodal distribution: It first goes up and then goes down, as illustrated in Figure 3.3 (Hannan and Freeman 1984, 1989). A well-received explanation is to draw on a causal mechanism regarding the liability of newness. When industries emerge, many firms will enter; however, the majority of them will fail early on due to inexperience, lack of resources, or legitimacy. However, for the firms that survive the first shakeout, they are likely to learn from their mistakes, to gain reputation and legitimacy, and to develop connections and adaptive capacity. The improvement suggests that the successful contestants are probably better, and their improvement will likely continue, implying a diminishing probability of failure over time.

Levinthal (1991) provides a simple, alternative explanation for the systematic pattern in Figure 3.3. His model assumes that all firms are the same: All share the same initial conditions as well as the same resource-cumulating process. That is, all start with the same resource endowment, and the resource cumulation follows a random walk: In each period, the resource increases or decreases by a value determined by the luck of the draw. Another assumption is that whenever a firm's cumulated resources touch a lower bound, the model assumes this firm as "failed," as if its performance is so low that it will go bankrupt. Figure 3.4 illustrates five firms' resource-cumulating trajectories, which follow the assumptions mentioned above.

As Figure 3.4 shows, the five firms' resource trajectories differ considerably. Nevertheless, all the differences were determined entirely by luck in this case. They started with the same endowment, which assumed to be one in this model. Then in each period, a value was drawn from a standardized normal distribution with the mean equaling zero and the standard deviation equaling one, which determines the resource gained (or lost) in a given period. A firm will cease to operate (i.e., fail) whenever its cumulated resources equal or are smaller than minus one. All surviving firms continue this resource-cumulating process. As Figure 3.4 shows, one of the five simulated firms (trial 1, the line with circles) obtained a cumulative resource smaller than minus one in period 9. It then failed, and its cumulated resource stabilized at minus one. Another firm (trial 2, the line with the x's) was very close to failing at period 21; however, it managed to bounce back and became the top-performing firm at period 50.

How can this fairly naïve model connect to the systematic failure pattern, as shown in Figure 3.3? To do this, based on the simulated data, we need to compute the hazard rate—the probability that a firm will fail at period t given that

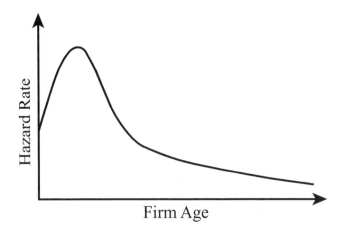

FIGURE 3.3 Hazard rate as a function of the firm age

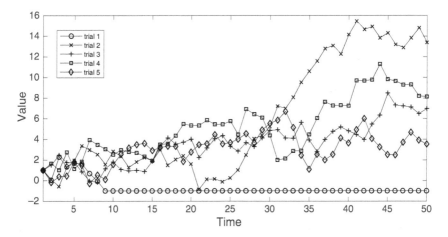

FIGURE 3.4 Five trajectories of resource-cumulating processes after Levinthal's (1991) model

the firm survived until period t - 1. We simulate ten million firms, each sharing the same initial condition as well as the resource-cumulating process as described above. We then compute the hazard rate for each period up to 50.

The result, as shown in Figure 3.5, reproduces the stylized fact shown in Figure 3.3. The hazard rate first increases, peaks at around period 4, then decreases down to period 50. The reason for the initial increase has nothing to do with the liability of newness. It is related to bad luck: Firms that happen to receive negative resources in the initial periods are likely to reach the lower bound and forced to exit. The reason for the later decrease in hazard rate has nothing to do with learning or improvement. It is related to early good luck: For the firms that did not fail early on, they are likely to cumulate sizable resources that will keep them further away from the lower bound, making them less likely to fail over time. Thus, a simple model based on a random walk process with a lower absorbing barrier (Denrell et al. 2015) can reproduce the empirical pattern and provide an alternative explanation.

Levinthal did not end his 1991 paper with a simple model illustration. He used the data from the Irish newspaper industry (typical setup shared by many studies of population ecology) to examine the extent to which the founding and failing patterns were consistent with a random walk model. In particular, he fit the data to the predictions by the null model (alternative, naïve explanation) as well as the learning model (existing explanation). The results provide strong support for the naïve predictions (i.e., luck is a better explanation for the unimodal hazard rate than the learning explanation). Importantly, the implication is not that the existing explanations are wrong, but they may be exaggerated in the presence of a simple, alternative theoretical mechanism that can also generate the observed empirical regularities.

Many different chance mechanisms can be used to build null models (Denrell et al. 2015), with a random walk mechanism being just one of them. Consider

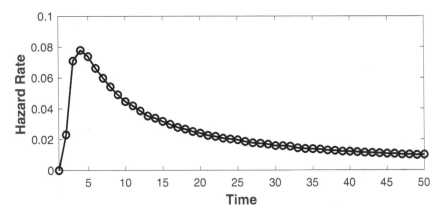

FIGURE 3.5 Hazard rate over time after Levinthal's (1991) model. The result is based on 10 million simulated firms

a chance explanation at a very different level of analysis: noise explanations of sub-additivity in probability judgments (Bearden et al. 2007; Hilbert 2012). It is an axiom of probability theory that the probability of mutually exclusive events cannot add up to more than one. Individuals asked to evaluate the probabilities of mutually exclusive events often give answers that add up to more than one (Fischhoff et al. 1978; Fox et al. 1996). Such sub-additivity in probability judgment has been examined extensively by experimental researchers and has typically been attributed to systematic cognitive bias. For example, it has been argued that events that are "unpacked" and described in vivid detail evoke multiple associations and are, therefore, overestimated (Tversky and Koehler 1994).

An alternative model assuming unbiased but noisy probability judgments provides a more parsimonious explanation (Bearden et al. 2007; Hilbert 2012). Suppose probability judgments are unbiased on average but subject to noise: The estimated probability of an event varies around the correct estimate. Consider the judgments of an individual asked to evaluate the probability of several mutually exclusive events. Because the probabilities of the different events add up to one, the average probability of each event has to be relatively small. For example, if someone is asked to evaluate five events, the average likelihood of these events is about 0.2. Because the true probability of the events being evaluated is close to zero, even unbiased but noisy estimates will, on average, lead to overestimation. The reason is a ceiling (or floor) effect: If the correct probability is 0.2, the event can only be underestimated by 0.2 at most but can be overestimated by a larger magnitude.

This model of noisy unbiased estimates can easily be tested empirically. The model predicts that overestimation is as likely as underestimation. Thus, the median error in probability estimates should be zero. In contrast, explanations of sub-additivity relying on cognitive bias predict that overestimation is more likely than underestimation. The re-analyses of past studies show that the model of noisy estimates explains much of the observed sub-additivity in probability estimates. When medians are used instead of means, there is still evidence for sub-additivity, although the magnitude of the effect is much smaller (Bearden et al. 2007). The model of noisy unbiased estimates provides another illustration of how chance (random but unbiased probability judgments) can credibly explain a phenomenon (sub-additivity in probability judgments). Luck in the sense of variability is key to this explanation. A model assuming unbiased estimates with no variability would not explain sub-additivity. The assumption that probability judgments are noisy is also well supported empirically (Faisal et al. 2008; Neri 2010).

In brief, the examples above highlight three features of the semi-strong version of quantifying luck using naïve models. First, one needs to understand the existing findings and explanations. In the Levinthal case, the unimodal hazard rate is well-known, and the learning explanation is well-received. In the probability judgment case, the systematic bias—sub-additivity—is widely recognized in experiments, with the dominated explanation being cognitive biases. Second, one needs to develop a naïve model by combining luck with plausible theoretical mechanisms. In the Levinthal case, a simple, cumulated random walk process with an absorbing barrier was assumed. In the probability judgment case, the assumption was regarding the barriers that bound the noisy probability estimates. The simpler the model, the stronger the impact when it reproduces the empirical regularities. Third, one needs to go beyond the naïve model and test the predictions against the data and existing explanations. The null model quantifies the impact of luck, and such hypothesized impact needs to be tested against data. If one can achieve all these three conditions, such as the cases of Levinthal (1991) and Hilbert (2012), a complete circle of quantifying luck using the naïve model approach is achieved. Other explanations need to provide stronger predictive power than this enhanced baseline before they can be considered plausible. Nevertheless, this approach has not yet diffused too much in management scholarship because it requires both the skills in computational models as well as skills in empirical or experimental analyses. Developing requisite skills for these tasks is non-trivial and time-consuming. A diverse research team is a likely solution when applying this semi-strong version of quantifying luck.

3.3 The strong version: luck as a regulating factor for judging merit

When top performers do better and how long their high performance endures are important questions in the management scholarship. Nevertheless, the weak and semi-strong accounts are not sufficient to address these important questions because both of them focus on generating a baseline that assumes no difference in merit among individuals or organizations.

Here I introduce the strong version of quantifying luck, which can help in answering the important questions above through the explicit modeling of the interaction between skill and luck. In many activities, performance is influenced by chance events beyond the control of individuals. Corporate success is influenced by fluctuations in exchange rates (Bertrand and Mullainathan 2001). The performance of product managers depends, in part, on whether they introduce new successful products, although product success is very difficult to forecast. Success in research depends on peers' evaluations, and promotions in organizations depend on superiors' subjective evaluations, although research shows that such evaluations are subject to substantial noise and bias (Feldman 1981; March and March 1977; Thorngate et al. 2008).

Researchers have also noted that such chance events do not necessarily average out over time. Persistent differences in performance will emerge if the underlying process is a random walk (i.e., one in which the noise terms are added over time) (Denrell 2004; Feller 1968; Levinthal 1991). In addition, processes of positive feedback may amplify initial chance events (Arthur 1989; Merton 1968). Because individuals with early success are treated differently, given more resources, offered specialized instructions, and expected to succeed, they become more likely to succeed. Similarly, if consumers choose products based on previous customers' recommendations, firms with initial good luck can end up dominating the market even if the quality of their products are not superior (Lynn et al. 2009), as illustrated in Salganik et al.'s (2006) experiment on music downloads on the Internet. Models of stochastic allocation processes, which incorporate the assumption of "positive feedback," have illustrated how it can lead to substantial and persistent differences among individuals and firms with identical skills (Arthur 1989; Barabasi and Albert 1999; Denrell et al. 2015).

If chance does play an important role in determining performance, what are the implications for performance evaluation, promotions, and learnings from others? Most commentators agree that if chance plays an important role, managers need to be cautious about attributing high performance to high skill. The general idea is that when performance is noisy and high performance emanates from luck rather than skill, high performance is not a reliable indicator of high skill. In an extreme scenario, if performance is only due to chance, high performers are not likely to be more skilled than others, and managers should not reward them or try to learn from them. March and March (1977) claim that if the careers of school superintendents are driven mainly by chance events, then "little can be learned about how to administer schools by studying successful high-level administrators that could not be learned by studying unsuccessful ones" (1977, p. 408). In a similar vein, Stinchcombe (1987), Barney (1997), and Cockburn et al. (2000) argue that little can be learned from case studies of profitable firms whose profitability is due to lucky bets on difficult-to-anticipate scenarios.

Figure 3.6 illustrates the view of how noise impacts inferences about merit or skill. In a system with low amounts of noise (i.e., no luck case, the light gray line), high performance is a reliable indicator of high skill, and low performance is a reliable indicator of low skill. As a result, the expected level of merit increases rapidly with increased performance. In a system with large amounts of noise

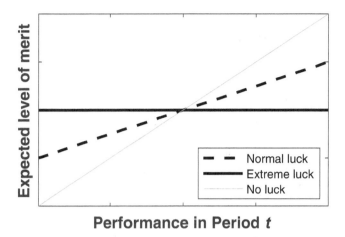

FIGURE 3.6 Performance associations based on three levels of the impact of luck

(i.e., normal luck case, the dark, dashed line), however, the correlation between performance and merit is low. As a result, the expected level of merit for high performers is only marginally higher than that for low performers. In an extreme scenario, in a system with only noise (i.e., extreme luck case, the dark, solid line), performance is not correlated with merit, and the expected level of merit is the same for high and low performers.

This view of the impact of luck (i.e., increasing unpredictability and making high performance a less reliable indicator of merit) is arguably the most common in the literature. It is also consistent with how the effect of noise is modeled and measured in papers that explicitly model the effect of luck on inferences of skills. The focus is on how luck and the mechanisms that amplify it reduce the correlation between ability and realized performance. For example, Lynn et al. (2009) examined how strongly reinforcing mechanisms can lead to a low-rank correlation coefficient between performance and quality. In particular, actors with a similar initial quality can obtain very different eventual social status when initial differences enable a run-away process in status cumulation. Similarly, Harrison and March (1984) examined how noise reduces the reliability of signals and the correlation between ability and performance.

An implicit assumption in the literature is that increased levels of luck reduce the positive correlation between performance and skill but does not reverse it. The implication is "higher-is-better": High performers are assumed to be more skilled, albeit perhaps only marginally so, than low performers. For example, in all the simulations in Lynn et al. (2009), the rank correlation between status and quality is positive, implying that high-status individuals are, on average, of higher quality than low-status individuals. Similarly, Starbuck's (2005) analysis of the extent to which publication in top-tier journals reveals about the quality of the paper shows that, regardless of what assumptions are made about the reliability of reviewers' judgments, papers in top-tier journals are likely to be of higher quality, albeit perhaps only marginally so.

The assumption that expected skill is monotonically increasing in the observed level of performance has important implications for how to interpret performance records, for selection and allocation of rewards, and for whom to learn from and imitate. If the association between ability and performance is weak but still positive, it makes sense to promote and learn from the highest performers. While the highest performers may be only marginally abler than others, they are still likely to be abler. The effect of noise, in this case, is mainly to reduce managers' confidence in the conclusion that higher performers have higher skills.

Here I show that a strong influence of luck can not only lead to a weak but also to a negative association between performance and ability (i.e., a "less-is-more" effect, which invalidates the higher-is-better assumption). That is, for moderate levels of performance, performance and merit are positively associated; however, for high levels of performance, the association reverses and becomes negative.

To demonstrate this possibility, consider a model of a repeated game. In such settings, streaks of high performance are usually considered impressive. The argument is that streaks of high performance—high performance during many periods—are unlikely to stem from luck but are an indication of superior skills. This argument, however, presumes that performances in different periods are independent. In many social settings and businesses, performances are seldom independent but often dependent: The level of performance in period t is often influenced by the level of performance in period $t - 1$. For example, high initial performance may be self-fulfilling (Merton 1948), or processes of increasing returns may favor actors or firms who have gained an initial advantage (Arthur 1989; Barabasi and Albert 1999; Denrell et al. 2015).

Previous research has illustrated how such dependency can magnify noise and lead to substantial decoupling between abilities and eventual performance. Actors and firms who are not necessarily of superior ability but get lucky initially may end up being dominant and obtaining high rewards. The implication is that high performance during many periods may not be a reliable indicator of high ability (Denrell et al. 2013).

Dependency in performance can also have another effect: Longer streaks of high performance may, in fact, be evidence of lower rather than higher ability (Denrell and Liu 2012). The intuition is similar to the reasoning above: Long streaks is an indication of strong dependency in performance, and in such situations, long streaks of high performance are not as impressive as in settings where performances are independent.

To illustrate the basic point, first consider a simple, transparent stochastic process: coin tosses. Imagine that someone tosses a biased coin n times. The goal is to obtain as many "heads" as possible, which will count as a success. However, individuals differ in their skill levels: Some individuals are more skillful than others in that they have a higher probability of obtaining heads in any given period. Stated differently, the coin is fair, and the "bias" in favor of "heads" differs among individuals.

In addition to being biased, I also assume that coin tosses in consecutive periods are dependent. The probability of obtaining heads increases if the previous outcome was heads. However, the level of dependence is not fully known. Thus, it is not clear whether a streak of heads is due to exceptional skills or strong dependencies combined with the good fortune of obtaining heads initially. In these circumstances, players who manage to obtain all heads will not be considered the most skillful. Rather, players with a moderately high number of heads obtained are the most impressive.

Model setup

Consider a population of players who toss coins n times. The probability that player i gets heads in the first toss is c_i. The probability of obtaining heads in subsequent tosses depends on the outcome obtained in the previous toss. If the previous outcome was heads, the probability of obtaining heads increases to $(1 - w_i) c_i + w_i$, where $1 > w_i > 0$ is a positive fraction. If the previous outcome was tails, the probability of obtaining heads decreases to $(1 - w_i)c_i$. Clearly, larger values of w_i imply that the process is more strongly dependent, in that success probabilities depend less on c_i and more on the outcome of the previous toss.

Here c_i is the skill level of player i and is equal to the expected proportion of heads obtained in the long run. We assume that players differ in the value of c_i: Some have a high value—corresponding to a high level of skill—while others have a low value. For modeling such dispersion in skills, it is assumed that the value of c_i is drawn from a talent distribution at the beginning of the game and then remains constant throughout all periods. In what follows, I assume that c_i is drawn from a beta distribution—a flexible distribution and a common choice for modeling heterogeneity in success probabilities.

Parameter w_i represents the strength of dependency in the process. It is assumed that the value of w_i differs among individuals. The idea is that individuals can be in different social settings, different markets, or make use of different strategies and that the extent to which success probabilities depend on past outcomes may vary because of this. To model such heterogeneity in the value of w_i, I assume that at the beginning of the game, parameter w_i is drawn from a probability distribution. As above, we assume that distribution w_i is drawn from a beta distribution.

Finally, I assume that the value of w_i is not known to outside observers. Thus, observers do not know whether there is a strong level of dependency in coin tosses. Stated differently, observers do not know whether the level of skill or past outcomes is most influential in determining success probabilities.

Model result

One hundred coin tosses by ten million players were simulated. Each player had a different value of c_i and w_i. In the simulations, I drew c_i from a beta distribution with parameters (10,10) and drew w_i from a beta distribution with parameters

(1,1) (i.e., w_i was drawn from a uniform distribution). These assumptions imply that skill distribution (the distribution of c_i) is more concentrated around 0.5 than the distribution of w_i.

Based on the simulated data, we can examine how success—the number of heads obtained—is associated with skill levels: the value of c_i. Intuitively, one might expect that players who achieved the most success are the most impressive. That is, players who achieved the largest number of heads have the highest value of c_i. However, as Figure 3.7 shows, the association between success and skill level is, in fact, non-monotonic. Figure 3.7 plots the average skill level; that is, the average value of c_i as a function of the number of successes obtained (i.e., the number of heads). As shown in Figure 3.7, the average value of c_i reaches a maximum of about 80 heads out of 100 and then starts to decline. Players who achieved 100 heads in 100 trials have an average value of c_i lower than those with 80 heads in 100 trials. Stated differently, the most successful players are not the most impressive. Rather, moderately successful players are the most impressive ones. A similar pattern is observed for very low levels of success: The players with the lowest level of success are not the least impressive.

The explanation for this result is the heterogeneity in the impact of luck. In settings where w_i is large, early luck is amplified, and outcomes depend more on luck than skills. For example, as illustrated in Figure 3.8, the correlation between c_i and the number of successes is only 0.41 when $w_i = 0.9$. The amplifying effect of w_i has two consequences. First, extreme results—achieving a very high or very low number of heads—will be more likely when w_i is high. Second, extreme results are not that informative mainly because when w_i is high, outcomes are less influenced by skill levels and more impacted by luck. Even a low-skilled player who happens to achieve success initially will likely have many successes when w_i is large. It follows that when w_i is large,

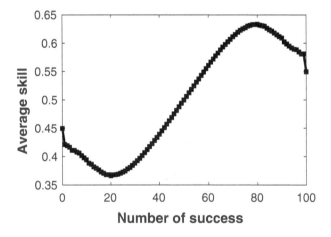

FIGURE 3.7 How average skill varies with the number of successes where the current outcome depends on both skill and previous outcome

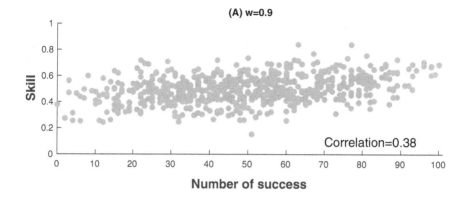

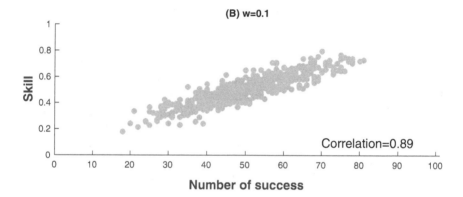

FIGURE 3.8 The distributions of skill versus success based on two values of w

achieving a large number of heads is not that impressive. That is, when w_i is large, beliefs about c_i should not be updated much because even a player with low skills could achieve a large number of heads.

In settings when w_i is low, on the other hand, the impact of luck is reduced, and skill levels play a crucial role in determining the outcome. For example, as illustrated in Figure 3.8, the correlation between c_i and the number of successes is 0.88 when $w_i = 0.1$. Because skills play a crucial role in determining the outcomes, outcomes are also more informative about skill levels. For example, achieving a large number of heads is a reliable indicator of high skill because it is very unlikely that a player with low skills would achieve this level of successes. However, as Figure 3.8 illustrates, a low value of w_i also implies that extreme performances—achieving a very high or very low number of heads—is less likely than when w_i is high.

Overall this approach illustrates the strong version of quantifying luck: One can infer the relative impact of skill and luck on performances. It not only accommodates the conventional understanding of luck—how luck weakens the association between performance and skill—but also provides a more counterintuitive insight: Luck can sometimes be so influential that it generates a negative correlation between success and skill. The implication is as follows: Extreme levels of performance are less likely when they are a reliable signal of high skills and more likely when they are a less reliable signal of high skills. Achieving 100 out of 100 possible heads indicates that the value of w must have been high, and in such settings achieving 100 heads is not so impressive.

3.4 Measuring the impact of luck using real-world data

The previous section demonstrated the strong version of luck using a formal model. The coin-tossing model demonstrates how a simple reinforcing mechanism can generate counterintuitive inferences about skill and luck. While the dynamics are straightforward, its dependent variable on inferred skill presents a challenge of linking it to empirical data because skill is difficult to be defined and measured in the real world.

In this section, I introduce an alternative approach that can address this challenge: One can examine the impact of luck by measuring the associations between current and future performances. Expected future performance and expected skill are two sides of the same coin in formal models, although consecutive performances are easier to measure in real-world data. To this end, we need to elaborate on the idea of regression to the mean, which allows us to extend the strong version of quantifying luck to empirical data.

Regression to the mean occurs whenever performances are not entirely under actors' control but are influenced by unsystematic factors (i.e., luck). Most observed performances can be attributed to one of two factors (Ross and Nisbett 1991): systematic factors (i.e., dispositional factors such as actors' traits, products' quality, or firms' routines) and unsystematic factors (i.e., luck). Higher performances can signal superior skill but also greater luck. Since luck is more changeable, higher performances tend to be associated with future performances that are expected to be lower than current performances, regressing downward to actors' mean performance (i.e., actors' skill). Specifically, regression to the mean suggests a systematic change between actor i's consecutive performances ($\mathrm{E}[P_{i,t+1} - P_{i,t}]$), providing the current performance ($P_{i,t}$) is greater or smaller than actor i's mean performance (μ_i if actor's mean skill is known or $\mu_{i,t-j:\ t-1}$, an estimated, moving average based on actor's available past performances up to period $t - 1$). Formally,

$$E[P_{i,t+1} - P_{i,t} \mid P_{i,t} > \mu_i] < 0 \tag{1}$$

$$E[P_{i,t+1} - P_{i,t} \mid P_{i,t} < \mu_i] > 0 \tag{2}$$

This formulation means that whenever actor i's current performance is greater than his or her mean performance, there is likely a systematic decrease across consecutive performances (i.e., future performance is expected to be lower than current performance). On the other hand, whenever current performance is lower than mean performance, there is likely a systematic increase between consecutive performances (i.e., future performance is expected to be higher than current performance).

To illustrate the effect of regression to the mean, consider the performances of elite athletes, such as Usain Bolt, the world record holder in the 100 meter sprint. During his career, Bolt achieved 71 sub-10-second 100 meter sprint.[4] Figure 3.9 shows the distribution, and his overall mean performance is 9.893 seconds. I apply equations (1) and (2) to his performances to demonstrate the effect of regression to the mean. That is, I compute the expected changes in performances for two categories of his performances: those smaller and those greater than his mean performance.[5] The expected change is negative (−0.0914) when Bolt's current performances are greater than his mean performance, and the expected change is positive (0.0909) when Bolt's current performances are lower than his mean performance. This suggests that regression to the mean occurs among Bolt's sub-10-second 100-meter sprint performances.

I then apply the same analysis to all athletes who had at least three sub-10-second 100-meter sprint performances ($N = 310$).[6] Similar to Bolt's analysis, each athlete has two conditionally expected changes, and Figure 3.10 presents the two distributions of these values. The results support a robust regression downward effect when current performances are higher than the athletes' own mean performances (upper graph) and a robust regression upward effect (lower graph) when performances are lower.

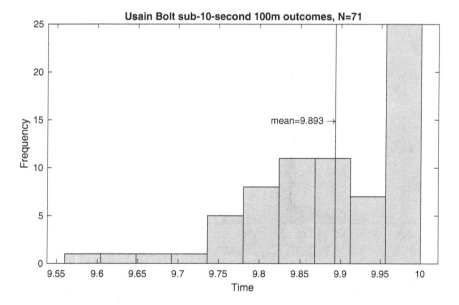

FIGURE 3.9 The distribution of Usain Bolt's sub-10-second 100-meter sprint performances

The illustrations of Figure 3.10 serve two purposes. First, the results show that even in a context where luck is generally believed to play a minimal role in outcomes, regression to the mean still occurs since the outcomes are not entirely under the athletes' control but can be influenced by unsystematic factors (e.g., tailwind). Second, this result implies that regression to the mean should hold in other contexts where luck is likely to play a greater role.

To examine this argument (i.e., the statistical regression effect is stronger when luck plays a greater role), we need a more general formulation than the one that focuses on regressing to individuals' own mean performances (Greve 1999). Samuels (1991) formalizes a weaker but more general property called "reversion toward the mean," which allows us to compare the regression effects across different actors and performance ranges. To explain this concept, suppose that u is the average level of performance in some population. Suppose we select the actors

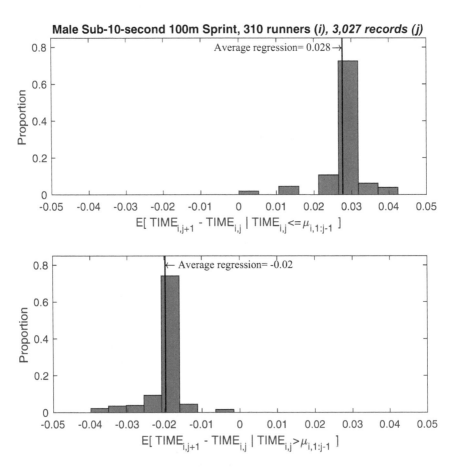

FIGURE 3.10 The distribution of regression downward effects (upper graph) and regression upward effects (lower graph) among all sub–10-second 100-meter sprint record holders

with a past performance above some cutoff $c > u$. Let $M_{c > u}$ be their average past performance, $M_{c > u} = E[P_{i,t} \mid P_{i,t} > c]$. Reversion toward the mean occurs when the expected future performance of these actors, $E[P_{i,t+1} \mid P_{i,t} > c]$, is lower than their average past performance ($M_c > u$). This can be generalized: If $c^+ > c^- > u$, then $E[P_{(i,t+1)} \mid c^+ > P_{i,t} > c^-] < E[P_{i,t} \mid c^+ > P_{i,t} > c^-]$, which suggests that for a selected group whose group mean performance is greater than the population mean, the expected future mean performance of this group will be systematically lower than this group's current mean performance even when the individual skill levels differ within the selected group. The other direction of the expected change also holds: If $u > c^+ > c^-$, then $E[P_{i,t+1} \mid c^+ > P_{i,t} > c^-] > E[P_{i,t} \mid c^+ > P_{i,t} > c^-]$. This formulation allows us to quantify regression to the mean across actors and performance ranges (see Figure 3.11 for an illustration).

Figure 3.11 shows four associations between current (t) and future performances ($t + 1$) based on varying assumptions about the underlying circumstances. First, if luck plays no role at all in performances, there will be no regression to the mean. This association is represented by the solid gray line (i.e., the 45-degree line). Current performance is a perfect predictor of future performance.

To illustrate an association that resembles a 45-degree line, consider university and business school rankings. In this context, luck may play a role for younger universities but not necessarily for the well-established ones. The rankings of the top universities, such as Harvard, Cambridge, or Oxford, are unlikely to fluctuate due to luck and are very persistent over time.

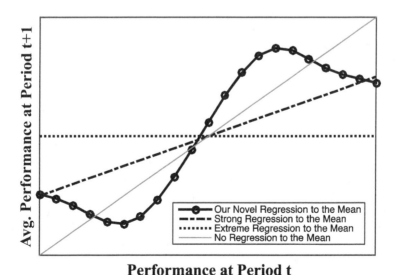

FIGURE 3.11 How future average performances vary with current performances with four different varying assumptions about underlying circumstances

The results, as shown in Figure 3.12, support this prediction. That is, the association for the top universities and Top 30 business schools is fairly close to a 45-degree line, suggesting a fairly weak regression to the mean effect. However, for the lower-ranked universities and schools, the association is still fairly close to the 45-degree line but also entails greater fluctuation than the top ones, implying that the impact of luck and regression to the mean effects are strong for lower-range performances.

On the other end of the spectrum in Figure 3.11 is the flat, dotted line. This represents the situation where performances are entirely determined by luck, and skill plays no role in outcomes. In this case, current performance is not a predictor of future performance at all. Expected performances should always regress to the overall mean performance across all performers.

To illustrate this, consider the lottery. When people consider situations where outcomes are entirely determined by luck, people usually refer to examples such as rolling the dice or tossing a coin. A real-life example concerns the winning numbers of lotteries. If it is truly random, then no matter what you observe in the past, it does not tell you anything about which numbers are more likely to win in the future. You should not use the past to predict the future at all. One can test if the results are truly random using the idea of regression to the mean. If it is a fair game and the numbers are indeed random, the association should be a flat line, centering around the mean of all possible numbers.

The results based on the US Wisconsin Powerball lottery, as shown in Figure 3.13, support this prediction. There are 59 balls in this Powerball lottery, so the mean is around 30. I collected the data from the official website; I also simulated the data based on the same game setup. The associations in both the real and simulated data are very close to the flat line, suggesting an extreme regression to the mean effect. There are more fluctuations in the real data because of a smaller sample size compared to the simulated data, which is based on one million trials.

Most performances we observe in reality should fall somewhere between the two extreme scenarios above. Skill plays a role in performances but so does luck. More extreme performances are expected to be followed by less extreme performances, regressing to the overall mean. This also suggests that the association between current and future performances should be flatter than the 45-degree line (due to the influence of luck) but also steeper than the flat line (due to the influence of skills), as represented by the dot-dashed line in Figure 3.11. If luck plays a strong role, extreme performances can indicate extreme luck, which is likely to entail disproportionally strong regression to the mean effect (Denrell and Liu 2012), as the solid line with circles in Figure 3.11 shows. Such disproportionate regression effects can generate a less-is-more effect (i.e., top performances are not only most regressive but become systematically worse than the less extreme performances).

To illustrate a less-is-more effect, I collected data from professional sports. Professional teams in the National Football League (NFL), the National Basketball Association (NBA), and Major League Baseball (MLB) cannot be too

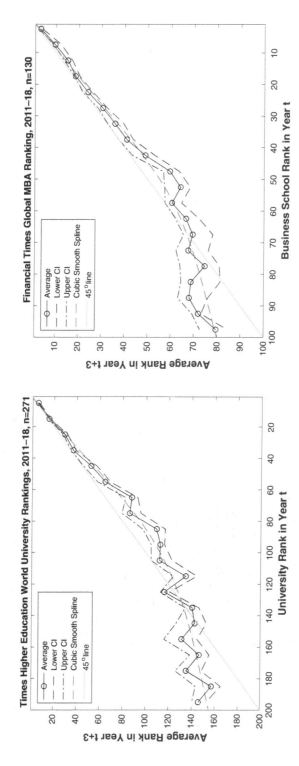

FIGURE 3.12 The associations of consecutive performances in World University Rankings and Financial Times Global MBA Ranking

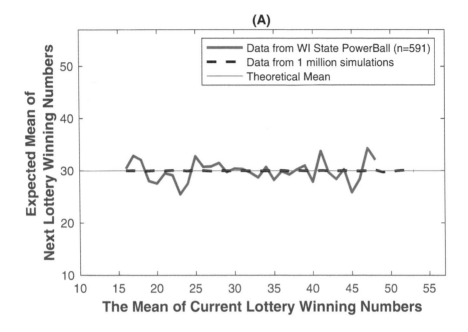

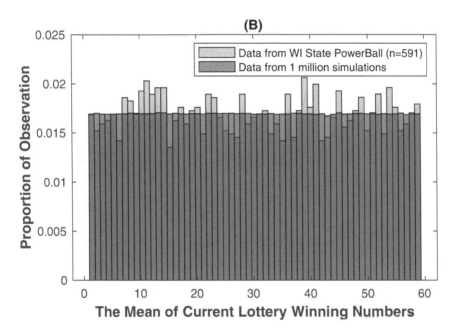

FIGURE 3.13 The associations of a consecutive winning number of (A) Wisconsin Power Ball lottery games and (B) simulated lottery games

incompetent—all players, coaches, and managers survived multiple rounds of competitive selections, suggesting that the "skill distribution" is likely pretty compressed. This suggests that the outcomes in these professional sports can be sensitive to factors other than skill: Not because teams are unskilled, but because they are all equally highly skilled. In particular, the winning percentages can be sensitive to a situational factor (i.e., the number of games played in one season). Regression to the mean effects are likely stronger, and less-is-more effects are more likely to occur in sports with fewer season games.

To examine this prediction, I downloaded the team performance data of these sports from their official websites (www.nfl.com, www.nba.com, and www. mlb.com). I then organized the data by computing the winning percentages of the same team in consecutive years. Lastly, I computed how the expected winning percentages in the next season varied with the winning percentages in the current season.

Figure 3.14 shows the results, with the solid line with circles being the average future winning percentages as a function of the current winning percentages for the same teams. The dashed lines are the confidence intervals based on 10,000 bootstrap simulations, and the light gray line is the 45-degree reference line.

Three observations can be drawn by comparing the results of the three professional sports. First, regression effects exist in all three sports with the effect being the strongest (i.e., the flattest performance association) in the NFL where the winning percentages are the least reliable due to a small sample size (16 games per season). Regression to the mean still occurs in the MLB; however, the effect is the weakest among the three due to a much larger sample size (162 games per season). Second, extreme performances are more likely to occur in the NFL than in the NBA than in the MLB. Extreme winning percentages (e.g., those greater than 80% or smaller than 20%) are almost absent in the NBA and the MLB but not in the NFL. This suggests that extreme performances are associated with performance unreliability due to a smaller sample size.

Third, the extreme performances in the NFL tend to regress disproportionately more to the mean in the next season, generating a less-is-more effect. In contrast, the associations between future and current winning percentages in the NBA and the MLB are monotonic without less-is-more effects. Even though performances regress to the mean in the NBA and the MLB, the relative rankings, on average, do not change over time. However, this is not the case in the NFL: Top (worst) performing teams in the current year tend not to be the top (worst) performing teams in the following year. Such a less-is-more effect tends not to be expected by a layperson who assumes performance monotonicity, and this has important implications for searching for strategic opportunities. I will return to this point using illustrations from sports betting in Chapter 4.

Next, can we find less-is-more effects beyond sports? For example, should we expect high-performing firms to continue performing better, or can the performance association also be non-monotonic?

To examine the extent to which rank reversals occur in a business context, I collected data on return on assets (ROA)—a widely used firm performance

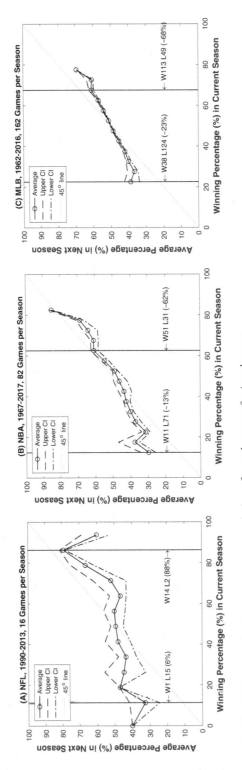

FIGURE 3.14 Season winning percentage associations from three professional sports

measure. The data were downloaded from the Thompson Reuters database and included all active US public firms from 1980–2010 with 7,147 firms in total during these 31 years. I computed the ranks of the firms by their ROA for each year. I first computed the firm performance ranks in year t. The expected rank was then computed for these firms in year $t + 1$, given their performance ranks in year t. To provide an overview of the changes in performance associations over time, Figure 3.15 shows nine-year pairs with a three-year interval from 1983 to 2008.

Figure 3.15 shows three notable trends in the ROA data from 1983 to 2008. First, there are strong effects of regression to the mean in all the year pairs examined. For example, a current year's performance rank of the 95th percentile tends to regress downward to the mean—to about the 80th percentile in the next year's rank. This regression effect holds in all year pairs; however, it is weaker for the lower performance ranks. For example, a current year's performance rank of the 20th percentile tends to regress upward to the mean—to about the 23rd percentile in the next year's rank on average. This means that higher performances (above median) are more regressive than the lower performances.

The second observation is that less-is-more effects do occur in the ROA data. In particular, the lowest performance ranks tend to regress upward to the mean more than the second-worst performance ranks in the 80s. Interestingly, this dip seems to move from the left end to the middle range over time. This suggests that performance unreliability was around the extremely low-performance range, but it has moved toward the middle-range performance over time, as indicated by the movement of the locations of the non-monotonic kinks.

The third observation is about the less-is-more effects in the high-performance range, which starts to appear from the 1998–1999 year pair. This holds for all the ten-year pairs examined in the 21st century, implying a systematic pattern. That is, top-performing firms (i.e., firms>95th percentile) tend to regress disproportionately more to the mean in the subsequent year than the second-best-performing firms (i.e., firms within 90th to 95th percentile), implying systematic less-is-more effects.

To further examine how persistent exceptionally performing firms are, Figure 3.16A illustrates how this unreliability has evolved over the past 30 years using the same ROA data of US public firms. A "persistence ratio" is developed by computing how many top 100 firms in year t are also the top 100 firms in year $t - 1$. For example, the persistence ratio is 0.27 in the year 2010, which means that only 27% of the top 100 firms in the year 2010 were also the top 100 firms in the year 2009. Figure 3.16A shows a trend of decreasing persistence from 1980 to 2011. This trend is consistent with the patterns identified in Figure 3.15—top-performing firms' performance regress to the mean during all year pairs examined; however, the effects of this regression had become very large since 1997 when the less-is-more effects occurred. These exceptionally performing firms' ranks dropped disproportionately more than the second-best-performing firms, leading to less-is-more effects at the highest performance range for all year pairs after 1997.

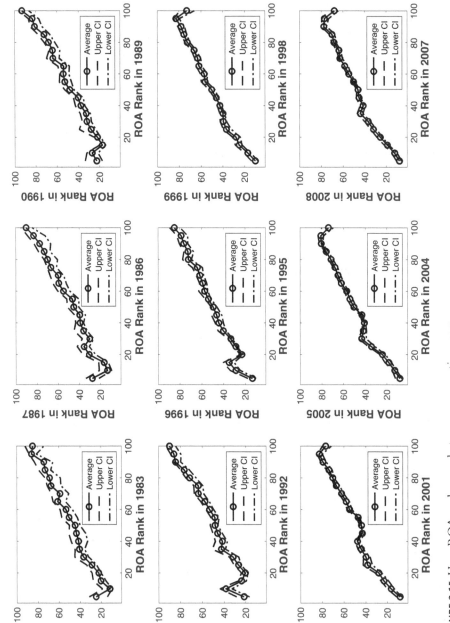

FIGURE 3.15 How ROA ranks vary between consecutive years

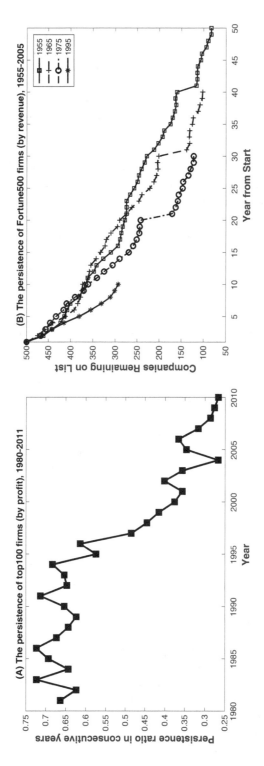

FIGURE 3.16 (A) The persistence of being the top 100 firms in consecutive years from 1980 to 2010 (30-year pairs); (B) the extent to which Fortune 500 firms persist on the list over time

Figure 3.16A shows a decreasing persistence in the profitability of US public firms. Figure 3.16B shows a decreasing persistence in revenue of large international firms. The result is based on an analysis of Fortune 500 firms. I downloaded the lists of Fortune 500 firms from their official website (fortune.com/fortune500) since the list was first created in 1955 and contained information up to 2005. The lists are based on the top 500 firms that have the highest revenue during that year. I measured the persistence of Fortune 500 firms by computing how many firms on a particular year's list remain on the list as time passes (I excluded the firms that changed names or were delisted due to mergers and acquisitions according to the information provided by fortune.com). Figure 3.16B shows the results based on four different starting years: 1955, 1965, 1975, and 1995. Note that in 1995, Fortune 500 decided to include service firms (such as Walmart and Citibank) on the list. This explains the significant gap in the number of firms for the three lines in Figure 3.16B starting before 1995 because several service firms began to have greater revenues than manufacturing firms.

The trends in Figure 3.16B are consistent with the pattern in Figure 3.16A: Exceptionally performing firms (both in terms of profitability and revenue) are losing or dying at an increasingly faster rate. In particular, the slope of the line based on the 1995 list is steeper than the other three lines in Figure 3.16B, suggesting that the turnover of the list is increasing over time. This implies a decreasing persistence of exceptional performances in terms of revenues.

I also explored how performance associations may vary across different industries and years. The patterns are less robust than those in Figure 3.15 because of smaller sample sizes in many industries. Here I report on three of the largest industries according to the Global Industry Classification (GIC) standard and the year pair of 2007/08 when a financial crisis occurred. The results, as shown in Figure 3.17, indicate strong regression to the mean effects in these three industries, although the non-monotonic performance associations vary among them. In particular, the performance association is relatively monotonic in the health care industry (Figure 3.17A), although it is non-monotonic in the finance industry (Figure 3.17C). Moreover, less-is-more effects only occur for the top-performing firms in the information technology industry but not at the lowest performance range (Figure 3.17B). This suggests that the effects of regression to the mean can be strong but idiosyncratic— contextual factors determine whether and where less-is-more effects occur.

3.5 Summary: what the luck?

I have introduced three versions of quantifying luck. The weak version is in line with the conventional way of building a baseline, null hypothesis by assuming that the outcome is produced by luck, such as sampling error. Systematic factors are favored when the observations are so extreme that they cannot be explained by the baseline (i.e., luck). The semi-strong version extends the weak version by building a more thoughtful naïve model, which assumes that randomness in a structured environment can produce systematic patterns. The null

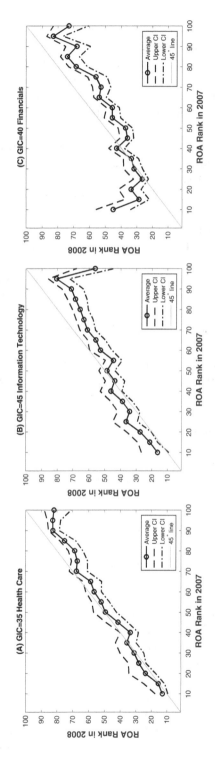

FIGURE 3.17 A selected sample of performance associations in 2007/08 year pair in three of the largest industry groups, according to GIC standard

model provides an alternative explanation when it can generate results that are consistent with the observed empirical regularities. Finally, the strong version addresses how to judge the relative impact between merit and luck across performance ranges. I used both formal models and data from the lottery, academia, sports, and business to demonstrate how the association between consecutive performances can help measure luck systematically.

The results show that the more extreme performances tend to regress more to the mean, and this regression is stronger when the performance is less reliable. The regression effects can sometimes be so strong that they generate less-is-more effects, such as in the NFL and the US public firm performances, although their impacts seem to vary. How does one make sense of these varying performance associations?

Here is a simple heuristic to make sense of the various associations shown: Their patterns depend on the interactions between the systematic factors (such as merit and skill) and the unsystematic factors (i.e., luck). If we assume performance is a combination of both these factors, depending on the distribution of luck, we can reproduce all the patterns discussed, as shown in Figure 3.18.

Figure 3.18A illustrates the default case: Regression to the mean always occurs when performance is not entirely determined by the systematic factors but also by luck. In this case, luck has an identical distribution to skill, and the association between current and average future performances are monotonic. Higher performances are regressive; however, the individuals or organizations associated with these performances are expected to have higher performances than others (i.e., a higher-is-better effect).

Figure 3.18B and Figure 3.18C introduce less-is-more effects. Sometimes, the impact of luck can be so strong that they generate non-monotonic associations, implying that high performers can perform systematically worse. However, as demonstrated, these less-is-more effects can happen in different locations because the impact of luck is context-dependent. When the highest performance is most sensitive to luck, the most exceptional performances are most regressive to such an extent that they have lower expected future performance. The top performers are likely those that benefitted from the successes of excessive risk-taking or their early luck being boosted by strong reinforcement mechanisms. Their future performances are extremely regressive because they are unlikely to be the luck of the draw again.

Figure 3.18C is related to extreme failures. For example, when a cascading failure occurs, even highly skilled operators may be overwhelmed because the system may generate additional errors faster than the operator can solve the existing ones. If this operator can perform again rather than being dismissed, such an extremely bad luck is less likely to repeat itself, making the extremely low performances most regressive. In contrast, the second-worst (i.e., those with low but not the lowest performance) should be a cause for concern. Their low performances suggest that extremely bad luck has not happened to them. Their low performances are informative about their low skill as well as low expected future performances.

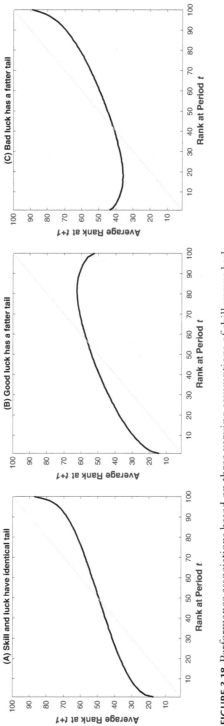

FIGURE 3.18 Performance associations based on three varying assumptions of skill versus luck

Overall, this chapter offered three systematic ways to model and quantify the unsystematic (i.e., luck). Each approach has its own intellectual history and applications. Readers can select the most suitable tools of quantifying luck, depending on the questions and contexts.

Notes

1 A necessary trick to ensure a sole winner is to announce that the guesses have to be different among the contestants in the final round.
2 One important difference between the actual and the simulated games is that I had to request different guesses among the final-round contestants to allow one single winner. This boosts the probability of obtaining one winner because it eliminates the chance of observing a zero winner and reduces the chance of observing multiple winners.
3 A more formal treatment of hypothesis-testing processes can be found in most textbooks of statistics.
4 Data for Figures 3.9 and 3.10 (all males' sub-10-second 100-meter sprint performances) were downloaded from www.alltime-athletics.com (retrieved on 12 November 2018).
5 The mean performance presented here is defined as moving averages: $\mu_{Bolt,\ t-j:\ t-1}$ with $j = 5$. The results hold if we use his overall mean instead, ($\mu_{Bolt} = 9.893$).
6 I acknowledge a selection bias of this illustration since I focus only on sub–10-second achievers, so the estimated mean performance may not reflect the athletes' true mean performance. This said, the athletes who achieved at least three sub-10-second performances are likely at the apex of their physical strength, and their mean performance should not vary too much across these performances. Thus, the moving average estimate may be a fairly reliable measure of their mean performance during career peak.

4

HOW TO STRATEGIZE
WITH LUCK?

No rational person would ever enter a lottery.[1] The chance of picking the right six numbers and hitting the jackpot in the UK's National Lottery is 1 in 45,057,474. However, even in something based purely on luck, a strategy can be found. If it was mandatory to play the lottery, how would you enhance your prospect of winning a larger payout? The answer: Always pick numbers above 31. This is because analysis has shown that the majority of people choose numbers associated with their birthday or a family member's birthday as their "lucky" numbers (Wang et al. 2016). Therefore, picking numbers above 31 will ensure that if your numbers are (luckily) chosen, you will get a much larger slice of the wins.

This example illustrates the key idea of this chapter: How to strategize with luck? By definition, luck is beyond our control and foresight because they are unsystematic factors. However, many studies have shown that people usually believe otherwise: They believe they can control luck in some ways; thus, they are fooled by randomness. More importantly, these luck biases are not unsystematic but predictable (Mauboussin 2012; Taleb 2001). Hence, the more informed strategists, like you, can utilize this knowledge and gain an advantage by exploiting your rivals' blind spots.

More generally, this kind of contrarian thinking can also be applied to businesses where strategy and behavioral science can be combined to exploit the many of our seemingly irrational biases. The idea is not new—smart traders have exploited the ways "noise traders" have been overreacting to news events for centuries (Barberis and Thaler 2003; Delong et al. 1990; Thaler 2015). This chapter will illustrate how taking advantage of others' biases is also feasible beyond the financial markets; that is, recognizing and fixing our own biases and then exploiting the biases of others can yield a successful strategy for business. How exactly you go about it requires solid evidence and analysis to provide a strong foundation for strategizing.

Hence, I call this approach "analytical behavioral strategy," in other words, drawing on behavioral science knowledge to search for contrarian opportunities and then utilizing data analytics to formulate a specific exploitation strategy to gain a competitive advantage. Here I intend to focus on the biases related to the ways people are fooled by luck and randomness.[2]

4.1 Rewarding and blaming people for their good and bad luck

How performance is perceived and attributed has important implications for strategizing. Decades of research in cognitive and social sciences suggest that people tend to be fooled by randomness and mistake luck for skill, particularly when evaluating extreme performances. Let us consider a concrete example adapted from Perrow (1984, pp. 5–7).

> Jack stays home from work because he has an important job interview downtown this morning that he finally negotiated. His wife has already left when he makes breakfast, but unfortunately, she has left the glass coffeepot on the stove with the light on. The coffee has boiled dry, and the glass pot has cracked. Coffee is an addiction for Jack, so he rummages about in the closet until he finds an old drip coffeemaker. Then he waits for the water to boil, watching the clock, and after a quick cup dashes out the door.
>
> When he gets to his car, he finds that in his haste he has left his car keys (and the apartment keys) in the apartment. That's okay because there is a spare apartment key hidden in the hallway for just such emergencies. But then Jack remembers that he gave a friend the key the other night because she had some books to pick up, and, planning ahead, Jack knew he would not be home when she came.
>
> Well, it is getting late, but there is always the neighbor's car. The neighbor is a nice old gent who drives his car about once a month and keeps it in good condition. Jack knocks on the door, his tale ready. But he told Jack that it just so happened that the generator went out last week and the man is coming this afternoon to pick up the car and fix it.
>
> Well, there is always the bus. But not always. The nice old gent has been listening to the radio and tells Jack the threatened lock-out of the drivers by the bus company has indeed occurred. The drivers refuse to drive what they claim are unsafe buses, and incidentally, want more money as well. Jack calls a cab from his neighbor's apartment, but none can be had because of the bus strike.
>
> Jack calls the interviewer's secretary and says: "It's just too crazy to try to explain, but all sorts of things happened this morning, and I can't make the interview with Mrs. Thompson. Can we reschedule it?" And Jack says to himself, next week he is going to line up with two cars and a cab and make the morning coffee himself.

Your instinct may tell you to blame Jack for being a reckless person. But hold on a second; what if I tell you this example is a simplified scenario based on what happened in the nuclear accident at Three Mile Island? In this example, a broken coffee pot (caused by Jack's wife's inattention) triggers a series of errors and unexpected delays culminating in Jack missing his interview. Charles Perrow, who studied the Three Mile Island disaster in detail, argues that blaming Jack is unjustified because Jack could not anticipate that his backup plans, including a spare key to the door, his neighbor's car, or the bus, were all unfeasible. Like the operators at Three Mile Island, Jack was "confronted by unexpected and usually mysterious interactions among failures. . . . Before the accident, no one could know what was going on and what should have been done" (Perrow 1984, p. 9).

To examine how people interpret this case, I conducted a survey and asked the participants what they believed the primary cause of failure was. Using the above example, Perrow suggests five causes and asks which is the primary cause of this accident or foul-up: (a) human error (such as leaving the coffee near the fire or forgetting the keys in a rush), (b) mechanical failure (such as the broken generator in the neighbor's car), (c) the environment (such as the bus strike and the cab overload), (d) the system design (wherein Jack can lock himself out of the apartment, a lack of emergency capacity in the taxi fleet), or (e) procedures used (such as warming up coffee in the glass pot at home, allowing only normal time to leave this morning)?

Most of our participants blamed Jack.[3] Of all the survey participants, 64% ranked "human error" as the primary cause, consistent with Perrow's prediction: "Generally 60 to 80 percent of accidents are attributed to [operator error]" (Perrow 1984, p. 9).

Such responses agree with much research from the attribution theory, such as the "fundamental attribution error" in which people wrongly blame the person for outcomes determined by situational factors (Nisbett and Ross 1980). This is one of the many biases that are in line with decades of research in cognitive and social sciences, which show that people make systematic mistakes in their attributions and predictions. Support for this idea is not only grounded in experiments on individual decision-making (Kahneman and Tversky 1973) but also comes from research on financial markets (De Bondt and Thaler 1985) and on how managers and external observers romanticize high performers (Meindl et al. 1985) and hire stars who eventually fail to continue to perform well (Groysberg 2010).

For example, people tend to ignore the effect of regression to the mean and instead predict future performance based on current performance as if the latter was a reliable predictor of the former. As discussed in Chapter 3, regression to the mean is a statistical phenomenon that provides a baseline, acausal account of performance changes. It is not incompatible with causal explanations for systematic performance changes. For example, performance decline may result from changes in the individuals involved, e.g., high performers may have reached their aspirations, thus investing less effort in subsequent tasks (Greve 2003;

Groysberg 2010). The decline can also be caused by changes in the circumstances. For example, high performances may attract competition and imitation (Barnett 2008; Peteraf 1993). The problem is that humans usually look for a causal mechanism for performance changes when the changes may be a statistical phenomenon that occurs in the absence of a causal mechanism (Kahneman 2011; Kahneman and Tversky 1973).

In his book published in 1933, statistician and economist Horace Secrist emphasized how competition *caused* the more successful firms to decline and the weaker ones to improve over time. He then recommended government intervention to avoid the predominance of mediocrity in American business. His findings and proposal were well-received in academia and government until a mathematical statistician, Harold Hotelling, pointed out that Secrist's finding is a mathematical necessity and his interpretation was a misunderstanding of regression to the mean (1933). Figure 4.1A reproduces a version of Secrist's finding using our data (see Chapter 3 for details). Using return on asset (ROA) as US public firms' performance measure, I plot how the average performance of five groups, based on performances in 1989, regressed to "mediocrity" over time. Is this regression toward the mean due to competition? Or is there perhaps a motivational explanation? For example, higher-performing firms become complacent and inert (Audia et al. 2000) while lower-performing firms become more alert or innovative (Christensen 1997). These causal mechanisms may be operating, but much of the observed tendency is likely due to the statistical tendency for the extremes to be followed by values closer to the mean. To bolster this claim, consider Figure 4.1B, which plots systematic changes in performance when time is reversed (Mauboussin 2012). We grouped firms into five groups based on their performance in 2010 and examined how their performances change going backwards in time. Again, a tendency toward mediocrity is observed. Such a systematic change cannot occur because performance in period $t + 1$ has a causal impact on motivation or competition in period t, but the statistical account is equally applicable when time flows in reverse.

To be clear, I am not arguing that existing causal explanations and management theories are wrong. I am arguing that their importance will be exaggerated if evaluators fail to take into account regression to the mean and how the statistical effects vary across performance distribution. More importantly, all these attribution and prediction errors suggest a luck bias: People can be rewarded for their good luck (i.e., the successes they do not deserve) and be punished for their bad luck (i.e., the failures they do not deserve), which, in turn, create profitable opportunities for the more informed.

4.2 Search guides for opportunities from the luck bias

The luck bias suggests that people are likely to misevaluate the values of high and low performers systematically, which provides opportunities for arbitrage (Denrell et al. 2019). In particular, the gap between the expectations and the

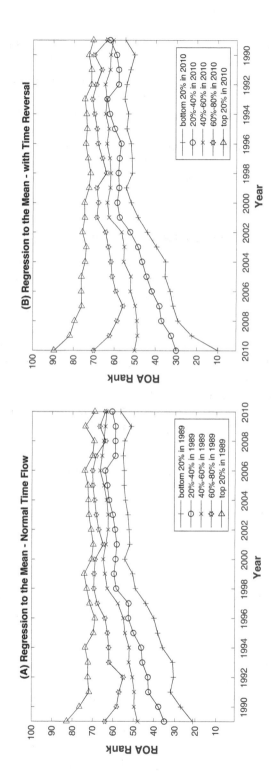

FIGURE 4.1 How performances regress to the mean under (A) normal time flow and (B) reversed time flow

actual value is the greatest for extreme performers, as illustrated by the less-is-more effects in the previous chapter. For example, top performers can have *lower* expected skill (and lower future performance) than the second-best performers, while naïve evaluators may believe that they will continue to perform brilliantly (and thus be willing to pay more than they should for acquiring this top performer). More importantly, arbitrage opportunities are more profitable when many people are evaluating in a similar but predictably biased way (e.g., by sharing the commonsense inference that higher performers are better). I will discuss how to arbitrage the misperceptions about good luck (for successes) and bad luck (for failures) below.

When some successes are too good to be true

Some successes are exceptional; however, what makes these successes exceptional is usually down to exceptional circumstances rather than exceptional merit. Therefore, one should attribute these successes more to the situations that enable them to be exceptional rather than to the persons that happen to be involved. I am not arguing that these exceptional performers are entirely unskilled. The problem is that people tend to over-attribute the successes to the dispositional factors of successful performers, thus giving them too much credit and reward. More importantly, naïve evaluators are likely to overestimate the values of successful performers and the likelihood that they could replicate their exceptional successes in other contexts. In these cases, informed managers can take advantage of other people's misevaluations of successful performers.

Avoiding the stars of others and disposing of your own

Exceptionally performing employees or business units are usually considered valuable assets. Sometimes their exceptional performances can continue if the context remains unchanged (e.g., a rich-get-richer dynamics is still present to boost the advantage). However, research has suggested that one should not expect an exceptional performance to continue for at least three reasons. First, the actors who achieve exceptional success will likely become overconfident due to self-serving attribution and hindsight biases. They may fall in the competency trap and become fragile when environments change. These biases make them more likely to make self-defeating errors. Second, the superior profit will likely attract competition and imitation. Finally, exceptional performance is generally expected to regress downward to the mean. Naïve evaluators are unlikely to recognize the three processes above; instead, they are more likely to romanticize successful individuals, neglect possible competition, and ignore regression to the mean. Thus, naïve evaluators are likely to predict that an exceptional performer is going to continue to perform exceptionally. This implies an overestimation of the value of a star employee, an organizational routine, or a business unit. An informed manager can do the opposite by avoiding hiring stars from other organizations or selling their own stars to the less informed counterparts to benefit from the misevaluation.

One well-known example is how Billy Beane, the manager of the Oakland Athletics in the MLB, avoided purchasing star players from other teams and occasionally sold his top-performing players to other teams (Lewis 2003). These top-performing players were probably skilled; however, their exceptional performance was reliant on a range of circumstances, which were not being factored into the evaluation. The Oakland A's were able to benefit from these "not buying high" and "selling high" strategies by not acquiring stars from other teams but trading their own stars with other teams who had an unwarranted high expectation of these "stars'" future performance. More generally, while "selling high" may be a riskier strategy because of its uniqueness, "not buying high" is a heuristic that most organizations should follow by default because of the systematic evidence that people tend to overestimate the stars and suffer from the winners' curse and disappointments when pursuing them (Thaler 2012).

Paying attention to the second-best

If one should not attend to the top performers of others (or reward one's own stars), then to whom should one pay attention? My theory suggests more attention should be paid to the second-best performers (as identified by the strong version of quantifying luck, see Chapter 3). Their less exceptional performances have two advantages for strategic arbitragers. On the one hand, their high but not very high performances indicate that they are less likely to achieve their performances in exceptional circumstances (otherwise they could have become top performers); therefore, one should attribute their performances more to merit rather than to situational factors.

Moreover, when the impact of luck is greater than the impact of skill, the expected skill is the highest for the second-best (see the previous chapter). On the other hand, the second-best performers may receive less attention from others because people tend to pay more attention to their higher-performing counterparts (i.e., the stars). This suggests that strategic arbitragers could acquire the second-best at a lower cost (probably several orders of magnitude less compared to acquiring a star) than their actual worth. Developing the second-best within one's own organization also helps—they may be surprised by the additional opportunities offered to them (which are normally allocated to the stars) and may develop a strong loyalty to the organization even when they become a star as a result of the arbitrage strategy.

This theory also has important implications for aspiration, learning, and imitation. There are systematic ways for a poor performer to improve and become a better performer. However, no rules exist for becoming the richest: To move from good to great depends more on being at the right place and the right time, such as grasping a rare opportunity and benefiting from the Matthew Effect to boost the initial fortune. However, people often imitate the most successful performers on the assumption that they are likely to be the most skilled (Strang and Macy 2001). Imitating the most successful performers could have been useful for our ancestors when the best performances were not so extreme that they could have provided a reliable indicator of high skill (Richerson and Boyd 2005). Modern technologies and globalization, however, could enable exceptional performances; these are so extreme that our heuristic of imitating the most successful performers fails systematically.

For example, many underperforming MLB teams learn from the most successful ones, such as the New York Yankees. However, rich teams such as the New York Yankees could afford to acquire the top-performing players and only retain the ones with the best skills. Moreover, winning is just one of the many goals for teams like the Yankees. Relative to teams based in smaller cities, the Yankees rely more on the revenues from corporate sponsorships and advertising. This means that the Yankees should acquire top-performing stars, not necessarily because the stars contribute more to future wins, but because the Yankees' important stakeholders (e.g., sponsors and fans) believe that top performers are the best. This implies that teams like the Yankees may learn that top performers are not necessarily the best, but they may behave as if they mistake luck for skill due to their reliance on the less-informed stakeholders. This example also implies that blindly benchmarking resource-rich teams such as the New York Yankees is likely to be detrimental to other teams. Learning from these salient successes seems to reassure the robustness of a winning formula, although it may be a formula that only works for the richest. Managers should, instead, learn from the less extreme performers (i.e., the second-best). The "second-best performers' practices" may be the most viable ones. Imitating these practices entails another advantage when few competitors are smart and brave enough to adopt the same unconventional strategy.

When some failures are beyond incompetence

Case studies of disasters have demonstrated that failures in organizations often result from a cascade of errors triggered by minor mistakes occurring in interdependent systems (Dorner 1996; Perrow 1984; Rudolph and Repenning 2002). Organizational researchers have argued that blaming the individuals in charge is usually unjustified in such cases because the fundamental causes of failures are tightly coupled systems, which render organizations sensitive to even trivial mistakes. Still, research shows that people in charge are usually blamed for failure (Coughlan and Schmidt 1985; Denis and Kruse 2000; Groysberg et al. 2004). How to exploit the ways people mistake bad luck for poor skill in these cases of misattributed blame?

Hire the fired and retain the failed

The discrepancy between the normative and descriptive accounts of responses to failures illustrates the existence of inefficiencies in the labor market: Competent actors can be dismissed for bad luck (Strang and Patterson 2014). The possibility of such inefficiency, in turn, suggests an arbitrage opportunity: Smart managers could hire, at a low wage, the individuals associated with failure. The fact that they failed perhaps indicates that they could have been more careful and cautious. However, the extreme failures they experienced are unlikely to have been brought about by their mindlessness alone. These unlucky managers are likely to suffer from stigmatization in the markets (Wiesenfeld et al. 2008). This suggests that informed managers could hire these underdogs with a lower wage than their intrinsic value.

Moreover, managers who are associated with failures should be retained rather than fired for two reasons. First, they are likely the unluckiest rather than the least skilled. Consider a skilled employee who happens to perform poorly in the first task assigned to him or her. This failure may cause his or her boss to form a negative impression of this employee and affect their future interactions, making the negative impression (and early bad luck) persist (Denrell 2005; Liu et al. 2015). Unless there are procedures to create interactions independent of attitudes, failures may be an unreliable indicator of low skill because competent actors can suffer from the enduring impact of bad luck: They may never have a chance to prove the evaluators wrong. Also, the failed individuals are likely to have had the opportunity to learn valuable lessons, helping them yield better results in the future. More importantly, if the company fires this manager and hires a new one, the firm is likely to engage in "superstitious learning," as discussed in the previous chapter. Encouraging the failed managers to exercise the lessons learned and make systems less tightly coupled can provide a more constructive way to improve performances and avoid the next "normal accident" (Perrow 1984). Second, failure can indicate that your employee is trying something new that may be worthy of encouragement. People who fail can suffer from others wanting to reduce their interactions with those associated with the failure. However, since good decisions can sometimes lead to failures and bad ones to successes, this is unlikely to be good practice. Companies will likely end up with the mediocre if they only select the successful individuals because candidates with impeccable records may indicate that they have never tried anything new but, instead, have mostly remained in their comfort zone. Overcome the success bias and "reward excellent failure" to enable the undervalued hidden gems for rejuvenating an organization.

Lastly, strategic arbitragers should pay more attention to the least popular products, individuals, industries, or firms. Popularity often has a self-reinforcing feature, particular after salient events. If an emerging industry happens to suffer a major bankruptcy, this failure can be so salient that investors and entrepreneurs will form an excessively negative impression, leading them to avoid further investments in this industry, which may otherwise be profitable. Recent research suggests that the occurrence of salient failure is the precise time to pay attention to those who enter this industry (Pontikes and Barnett 2017). Those who choose to enter this industry may be the ones who are viable enough to overcome the negative evaluation, and the competition will be less intense for them to realize superior performance. In contrast, most entrepreneurs and investors are attracted to industries where salient successes occur; however, those who jump on the bandwagon are less likely to succeed. The implication is that an arbitrager should pay attention to the events to which people tend to overreact, and then the arbitrage opportunity is likely to arise from a contrarian approach: avoiding the most popular individuals, firms, or industries and embracing the least popular ones.

Disposing of the second-worst performers

The second-worst performances should be a cause for concern for organizations, as discussed in the previous section. Nevertheless, many organizations cite their performances as a success because hardly any disasters have happened (Dillon and Tinsley 2008). Many modern organizations are complex systems, and a common feature of complex systems is that many hidden, interdependent interactions exist, which transcend the foresight and control of the managers who run the systems. This suggests that a small error or shock can diffuse without being noticed, creating a cascade of errors. When a cascade of errors occurs, additional errors may be generated faster than operators and managers can fix them (Rudolph and Repenning 2002). Even skilled managers may be overwhelmed by the situation.

In contrast, the second-worst performances in complex systems are likely to indicate that a cascade of failures did not occur (otherwise a disaster should have ensued). This implies that most observed errors are likely to result from operators' and managers' incompetence (e.g., failing to identify or fix the errors). Retaining these mindless managers in the organization is dangerous mainly because next time they may not be equally lucky, and their errors may escalate and create grave problems.

So, what should organizations do with the second-worst performers? On the one hand, organizations could release these second-worst performers, ideally to other organizations that overvalue their experience and expertise. Managers who have experienced "near-misses" are often wrongly portrayed as "heroes" because people focus on an unrealistic counterfactual scenario in that the situation could have been worse if these managers did not make certain decisions or take specific actions. Also, information about "near-misses" is often unknown to other organizations (Starbuck and Farjoun 2005). Organizations could exploit this near-miss bias and information asymmetry and dispose of the second-worst performers. These performers may be willing to move because other organizations may offer them a fresh start and a better package due to their lack of insights into these performers' previous near-misses. On the other hand, organizations should allocate more resources to develop and train these second-worst performers (rather than the worst performers) if they cannot be easily removed. These second-worst performers, if left to their own devices, are likely to trigger another round of error cascades (and hence disasters); therefore, organizations should spend more time and resources on improving their skills and mindfulness.

Proof of concept

To demonstrate the proof of concept of this approach to exploiting other people's luck biases, I revisited the context of the sports examples from previous chapter (the NFL versus the NBA). This is one of the contexts where limits to arbitrage inefficiencies are weak: One can exploit the luck bias as long as one can afford the bet.

The results are shown in Figure 4.2 with the solid line with circles showing the average future winning percentages as a function of the current winning percentages for the same teams. The dashed lines show the confidence intervals based on 10,000 bootstrap simulations.

The results from both the NFL and NBA show regression to the mean effects; however, less-is-more effects exists in the NFL. The results indicate the possibility of an opportunity. To illustrate this point, I downloaded the bookmaker odds historical data from www.oddsportal.com. I then identified the highest- and lowest-performing NFL teams in each year, whose current and future performance associations are most likely to entail less-is-more effects. I then simulated various investment portfolios based on bets on the salient winners' future season games to lose and on the salient losers' future season games to win. The idea was to exploit bookmakers' underestimation of salient losers and the overestimation of salient winners. The simulation results show that the investment portfolios have a positive return when the bet focuses only on the first game in the next season. This is not surprising in hindsight—bookmakers adjust their odds based on the observed performances during a season; therefore, the odds become increasingly reliable and reflect the actual competence of the team (against its rivals) over time. However, information about team competence is very ambiguous before a season starts. My findings suggest that the estimations may have anchored more in last season's outcomes, making the mispricing and behavioral

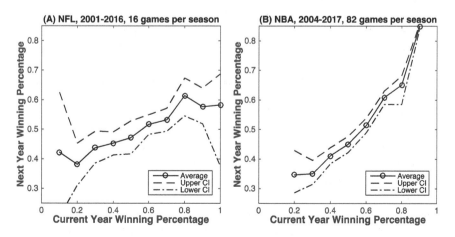

FIGURE 4.2 Performance association in (A) the NFL and (B) the NBA

opportunities more likely to exist. Interestingly, this exploitation strategy works even better for betting on salient losers' first season game to win. The reason is not because these underdogs are more likely to win, but because the odds are more favorable (e.g., 10/1 if the worst-performing team from last season won this season's first game) than for a similar strategy that focuses on the salient winners (e.g., 3/1 if the top-performing team from last season lost this season's first game). Stated differently, this strategy of exploiting other misestimations works more effectively when the focus is on the underdogs rather than on the stars because the degree of underestimation is greater than the degree of overestimation. One possible explanation is people's asymmetrical attention to winners versus losers: Winners attract more attention and scrutiny, so their odds can be overestimated but not to the degree of underestimating losers. Overall, this exercise shows that the findings of less-is-more effects are not merely theoretical artifacts but can be translated into a behavioral insight that promises superior profit.

4.3 Everyone is fooled by randomness, except you?[4]

Not all individual- or firm-level biases result in attractive behavioral opportunities. A mistake almost anyone can detect and take advantage of is unlikely to remain an attractive opportunity or provide a competitive advantage. In the same way that entry barriers protect attractive industries, and imitation barriers protect attractive resources, behavioral barriers protect attractive opportunities based on biases. Two classes of socio-cognitive forces, learning and legitimacy, are outlined here, which act as barriers to attempts to exploit a given behavioral opportunity.

The idea of exploiting other people's biases, discussed in the previous section (including the sports betting example), assume no competition except that the focal strategist can recognize and exploit the luck bias. If such a competition existed, the profit opportunities would be reduced or eliminated. Whether a behavioral opportunity is attractive or not depends on how many (and how well) rivals suffer from luck bias (such as ignorance of regression to the mean) and whether those who are free from the bias also try to exploit the same behavioral opportunity.

Figure 4.3 illustrates how the profits from exploiting the misattribution of luck depend on competition. Figure 4.3A focuses on the scenario in which a strategic resource is undervalued due to recent poor performance. Suppose most firms do not understand the luck bias, particularly the idea of regression to the mean. The common prediction then fails to take regression to the mean into account and will underestimate the value of the resource (and its complementary resources). The sophisticated unbiased prediction takes regression to the mean into account. The difference between the biased common prediction and the unbiased one is the potential profit the sophisticated strategist A can earn (on average) by acquiring the resource. If rival strategists also understand regression to the mean, they will also bid for the resource. The realized profit is the

FIGURE 4.3 The source of profit from exploiting the common misattribution of luck

difference between the highest bid from a rival strategist, which is the price strategist A has to pay to acquire the resource, and the unbiased prediction. All profits may be eliminated in the presence of a single competing bidder (Bertrand competition). In general, one would expect that a larger number of competing bidders will reduce the realized profit by increasing the price strategist A has to pay for the resource. Figure 4.3B illustrates the effect of competition when strategist A owns a resource (or its complementary resources) overvalued by others. Again, the presence of rivals who also own the resource and wish to sell it to naïve actors who overestimate its value will reduce profits (e.g., copycat tool shops during the Gold Rush). In this scenario, the presence of competing sellers implies that strategist A will have to sell the resource for a lower price than otherwise for lower profits.

The fact that the profit from exploiting misattribution of luck is larger when few firms understand and try to exploit regression to the mean implies that strategists should search for contexts in which barriers prevent the entry of competing firms. The basic argument is similar to the idea that entry barriers protect attractive industries and that strategic resources are protected by isolating mechanisms that deter comprehension and imitation (Rumelt 1984). Such barriers make it more difficult for firms, in general, to take advantage of an opportunity, making the opportunity more valuable and more likely to exist for firms that can overcome the barriers. While much of the strategy literature has focused on economic barriers that preclude imitation and entry (such as patents and economies of scale), opportunities can also be protected by behavioral barriers, including difficulties of learning and problems of coordination and legitimation (Oliver 1997).

Behavioral theories can help predict when there is less competition and hence more attractive behavioral opportunities. Two classes of behavioral barriers are discussed: learning barriers and interdependency barriers, drawing from two prominent, behaviorally grounded strands of literature (organizational learning and institutional theory, respectively). Many other constraints in learning and social interactions can build strong behavioral barriers. Here the focus is on the ones most relevant to the focal bias of misattribution of luck.

The learning barrier

The difficulties of learning moderate the extent to which evaluators could understand regression to the mean and, in turn, predict the attractiveness of a behavioral opportunity. Learning processes involve updates of beliefs (staying the same, reinforced, or revised), and the sources that trigger the updates can be a direct experience, the experience of others, or how these direct and indirect experiences are interpreted through evaluators' conceptual frameworks or paradigms (Levitt and March 1988).

A strategist is unlikely to profit much from a misevaluation of luck if competitors can easily learn from experience to make accurate predictions. Suppose rivals initially underestimate the value of a resource, but it is easy for them to learn from experience to revise and accurately value the resource. It follows that any profit opportunity will be eliminated if learning from experience is easy. In contrast, if learning from experience is difficult (or even superstitious), in that rivals are unlikely to learn to value the resource accurately, mistaken predictions can persist for a long time, and the rewards from exploiting misattribution of luck are likely larger because the differences between rivals' predictions and the unbiased predictions persist longer.

This argument implies that a strategic opportunity is likely to be more attractive if that bias is larger and/or it will last longer in settings where learning is difficult. When is learning more difficult? This is partly determined by whether the learning environments are "kind" or "wicked"—a distinction developed in the literature of judgment and decision-making (Hogarth 2001). A kind learning environment involves the necessary conditions for accurate inferences (such as uncensored data, speedy/reliable feedback, stable task environment), while a wicked learning environment invites flawed inferences (such as polluted data, sporadic/unreliable feedback, fleeting task environments). The literature on organizational learning has identified several settings, including noise, interdependencies, and competence traps in which learning from experience is unlikely to quickly identify the business practice with a higher level of payoff (Cyert and March 1963; Denrell and March 2001; Levinthal and March 1993).

In many settings, the learning environment is less kind; for example, limited data may be available. As a result, an evaluator who does not take regression to the mean into account will not have sufficient evidence available to conclude that her predictions were inaccurate. Such an evaluator may continue to underestimate an actor with poor past performance for a substantial period until sufficient data become available. Lack of data is especially problematic for less-is-more effects. The non-monotonic association occurs at extreme levels of performance and cannot be reliably estimated unless considerable data are available. Consider, for example, failures in complex systems, such as nuclear reactors. A skilled operator may be able to repair failure if it occurs in an isolated part of the system. If a failure occurs in an interconnected system, additional errors are triggered before a skilled operator can fix the existing ones. This suggests that catastrophic failures, which occur when a chain of failures is set in motion, may be less indicative of poor operator skills. Rather, they can be more indicative of the fact that failure occurred in a fragile part of the system. It is, thus, possible that operators associated with minor errors, which perhaps could have been preventable, are (on average) less skilled than operators associated with catastrophic errors, which can seldom be prevented. However, since catastrophic failure is a rare event, it is difficult to test this theory and reliably estimate the skills of operators associated with catastrophic failures.

Data may also be subject to selection bias. For instance, second-period performances may not be available for actors with poor first-period performances as they are less likely to participate again. For example, employees with poor initial performance, who are believed to be unskilled, may be dismissed or assigned to tasks in which performance does not depend much on their skills. If no data on second-period performances are available for actors with poor initial performances, an evaluator may continue to underestimate such actors. Because data are available on second-period performances of actors with high first-period performances, the evaluator will be able to observe that their performances regress to the mean. Such a reduction in performance, however, may be blamed on laziness or complacency.

It is important to note that the availability of data does not change whether regression to the mean occurs but impacts on whether a strategist can detect regression to the mean and accurately estimate its magnitude. It is easier to detect regression to the mean if considerable comparable data are available. As a result, behavioral opportunities are less likely to persist in large data settings. Limited data (such as mergers and acquisitions performances in niche industries) increase the chance of regression to the mean remaining undetected but also make it riskier to exploit such an opportunity because a strategist does not know the magnitude of regression to the mean or if it even exists. If sales have been exceptionally high, a strategist may expect regression to the mean but cannot precisely estimate the net present value of a firm without comparable data. Thus, data availability impacts on both the persistence of behavioral opportunities and the risks of exploiting them.

Regression to the mean can also be difficult to detect if skills improve over time. Competence usually improves more rapidly initially and then slows down (Argote and Epple 1990). The initial improvement in competence can offset the statistical regression effect, making the performance appear to be non-regressive. When actors' competence reaches a plateau, performances will start to be regressive again. Understanding and estimating the magnitude of regression effects are challenging in such a setting because observed performance changes can result from both changes in skills and regression to the mean.

Finally, learning can also be moderated by various interactive, socio-cognitive forces. For example, regression to the mean may appear to be weak when it interacts with other social biases, such as stereotyping (Fiske and Taylor 2013). Employees who fit the favorable stereotype are more likely to be hired and given additional resources. Their successes can reinforce the stereotype. For instance, systematic changes in performances may appear to apply only to counter-stereotypical employees; however, these changes are likely attributed to their negative stereotypes (such as laziness) instead of regression to the mean. Since the explanations may fit managers' conceptual frameworks, paradigms, or even prejudices, organizations may evaluate this performance feedback less critically, increasing the chance of failing to recognize the mistakes (Jordan and Audia 2012). Effective learning is difficult when socio-cognitive forces tend to reinforce rather than correct flawed beliefs. The current theory, then, predicts that these learning barriers can create attractive behavioral opportunities.

More generally, the idea that difficulties of learning can sustain competitive advantage is not new. For example, causal ambiguity in competency-based advantage can build barriers to imitation (Reed and DeFillippi 1990), and the sustainable advantage of a firm can occur when rivals continue employing sub-optimal strategies that are self-confirming (Ryall 2009). Here the focus is on the challenges of learning about regression to the mean and how they help the search for an alternative source of strategic opportunity.

The interdependency barrier

A strategist who wishes to take advantage of a strategic opportunity can often only do so by convincing and cooperating with others, such as employees and shareholders. The strategist must convince stakeholders that an opportunity exists in which it is worth investing time and money. Yet explaining and motivating stakeholders to adopt a strategy is more difficult when the strategy is unique (Benner and Zenger 2016; Litov et al. 2012). Explaining and motivating people in favor of a unique strategy is especially problematic for a strategist who wishes to take advantage of a behavioral opportunity. A behavioral opportunity exists because many people are biased and hence under- (or over-)estimate the value of a resource. The irony is that the bias that underpins an opportunity also makes it difficult to take advantage of it. That is, if most stakeholders, including shareholders and employees, suffer from the same bias, the strategist may have a difficult time explaining and convincing these stakeholders that an opportunity exists because it violates "cognitive legitimacy" (Suchman 1995).

Consider the case of an employee who initially performed a task very poorly. The commonsense prediction is that this employee is poorly skilled and will continue to perform equally poorly. Suppose that most employers make this commonsense prediction and underestimate the performance of this employee. A sophisticated strategist may offer the employee a salary that is slightly higher than what most other employers offer this employee. Also, suppose that the strategist has to motivate the board or other employees in favor of this hiring decision. If the members of the board or the employees do not take regression to the mean into account, they may fail to comprehend this strategy and object to hiring an individual with poor past performance. They may attribute this hiring decision to favoritism (the strategist has some personal reasons for hiring this employee) or simply poor judgment.

Even if members of the board or employees personally understand regression to the mean, they may argue that it would be difficult to explain to others, including customers, the decision to hire a poor performer instead of other applicants. For example, if the firm is involved in consulting, customers may care about the employees' track record because customers use the consultants' track record to infer their competence. If customers do not understand regression to the mean or simply do not have the time or data available to examine if the naïve prediction works well or not, customers may rely on the simple heuristic that future performance usually equates to past performance. As a result, customers may resist working with consultants with poor past performance. Knowing this, employers may resist hiring individuals with a poor track record, even if they personally suspect that the performance of these poor performers will regress to the mean. More generally, whenever outcomes depend on the reactions of others, people may refrain from acting upon a correct inference when they are uncertain whether others have reached the same conclusion. Instead, they may compromise and use conventional ways of evaluating actors, for example, by relying on past performances to predict future performances even if they privately know that such a prediction is an unreliable or biased estimate of actors' quality (Correll et al. 2017).

The fact that strategists may avoid exploiting a biased evaluation out of fear that others will misunderstand such a strategic move or interpret it as a sign of incompetence implies that the opportunity is more likely to persist if such an interdependency barrier exists. If there is no barrier of this type (i.e., when all actors who understand the opportunity can exploit it) and there is no need to convince and cooperate with others, the opportunity is likely to vanish quickly. In contrast, if few actors can exploit it, the opportunity is likely to persist longer. The opportunity is also more likely to be attractive for those who can take advantage of it because there is less competition.

More generally, behavioral opportunities are contrarian in nature, and doing things differently is usually associated with other people's misunderstanding, disapproval, and backlash (Gavetti 2012; Oliver 1997). Many other social dynamics not discussed here, such as conformity or institutional forces, can also deter evaluators from expressing what they personally believe. A common feature of these dynamics is that the social cost may overwhelm the economic benefit of exploiting a behavioral opportunity. This is bad news for market efficiencies (e.g., resources may be systematically mispriced due to factors unrelated to merit). However, this is good news for the strategists who are ready to exploit other people's mistakes— the stronger these behavioral barriers are, the more attractive these behavioral opportunities are for the strategists who can overcome these barriers.

Finally, one might argue that the arbitrage approach of exploiting others' mistakes is morally reprehensible (Akerlof and Shiller 2015). However, arbitrage is essential for eliminating market mispricing and inefficiencies. Without arbitrage, biases and inefficiencies are more likely to persist in the long term. Strategic arbitrageurs take market inefficiencies as given, and their activities are likely to debunk flaws in mainstream evaluations more effectively and allow merit to determine pay and career prospects in the long run, as the case of *Moneyball* illustrates. Strategy as behavioral arbitrage may be a surprisingly powerful instrument to overcome labor market inefficiencies.

4.4 Strategies of overcoming barriers to exploiting rivals' luck biases

Attractive opportunities from misattribution of luck exist when strong behavioral barriers protect the opportunities. Behavioral theories can be normatively useful because they not only illuminate an alternative source of profit (e.g., mis-pricing due to a common bias, such as ignorance of regression to the mean) but also predict when the bias creates a more attractive opportunity (e.g., fewer rivals can recognize or act upon the opportunity due to learning or interdependency barriers). However, the behavioral barriers collectively pose a paradox: Attractive opportunities from other people's misattribution of luck most likely exist in contexts where they are also most challenging to detect, learn, and act upon. Why is it that some strategists can succeed in exploiting strategic opportunities while others fail? Behavioral theories can also help illuminate how a strategist could exploit these opportunities more effectively than the rest.

How to become less dependent on others

To exploit a behavioral opportunity, a strategist should first examine whether he or she can be in a position to overcome the interdependency barrier. Behavioral opportunities protected by interdependency barriers will be especially valuable for strategists who can ignore social constraints and who are less dependent on convincing and gaining the approval of others. If a strategist needs resources from others (e.g., financial or social support) to implement his or her strategy, the strategist is then constrained by whether these stakeholders endorse the strategy (Barney 2018; Pfeffer and Salancik 1978). Stakeholders may withdraw their support if the strategy is based on regression to the mean, because stakeholders may fail to comprehend it. In contrast, a strategist in a private firm does not have to convince the shareholders about the benefits of a strategy and may thus be able to take advantage of opportunities unavailable to others. On the other hand, a company that sells advice to customers has to explain why their advice would lead to improved efficiency for customers. Contrast this with a company that is involved in production; this company can implement the advice and produce a product with increased efficiency without having to explain to outsiders why this procedure would work.

More generally, there is a continuum of the level of dependency, and the financial market represents the lower end. For example, opportunities in stock markets are often created by noise traders' suboptimal investment strategies (Delong et al. 1990). Traders can pursue these opportunities swiftly whenever they are identified. However, traders are not entirely free unless they invest with their own money. Otherwise, traders can lose capital support from their funders if the trading strategies of the former are too sophisticated for the latter to understand (Shleifer and Vishny 1997). This interdependency constraint is greater for strategists outside of the financial markets—they can lose capital, resources, and social support if their stakeholders fail to comprehend their strategy, misinterpret the exploitation tactics, or discount the outcome for its uniqueness.

We suggest that strategists should focus their search for opportunities in settings where they are less dependent on others than their competitors are if such settings exist. For example, a firm with low status and few applicants for new positions may not have to justify why they hire someone with poor past performance. Strategists may also need to reduce dependency on others before pursuing a behavioral opportunity. One way to reduce dependency is to ensure that outcomes are objectively evaluable. For example, a strategist who acquires an undervalued resource is less likely to benefit from the resource if its future contribution is difficult to evaluate. The ambiguity may lead the stakeholders to stick to their previous underestimation. This suggests that strategists should evaluate whether the misevaluated resources, once acquired, can unambiguously generate value. For example, private equities' due diligence usually takes into account whether the acquired firms' performances can be improved, along with metrics that potential future buyers could understand, such as by obtaining higher market share or return on assets/investment. This enhances the chance of a successful exit and positive return.

Next, a strategist should search for behavioral opportunities outside his or her immediate network. The interdependency barrier is stronger in interconnected cliques. This poses a dilemma in that a learning barrier may be easier to overcome within networks because the information is more readily available to those already in the networks than it is to outsiders who might want to profit from it. However, the interdependency barrier predicts that this is also an occasion when unusual actions may attract stronger resistance. Potential returns to carrying out unusual actions can be outweighed by the penalty associated with deviating from local norms. This implies that strategists should reduce dependency by seeking misestimation in remote, less constrained parts of their networks.

Third, strategists can also proactively distance themselves from stakeholders who are bounded by norms. Consider Michael Burry, a fund manager and the main character in *The Big Short* (Lewis 2011), who set up his office far away from the financial centers and turned off Bloomberg news updates to maintain his natural state of being an outsider. By reducing exposure to norms, incumbents, and noisy information, a strategist is more likely to judge an opportunity based on its merit rather than social norms. While interdependency barriers can be attenuated by being an outsider, outsider status creates other challenges, such as understanding what resources are misevaluated (i.e., learning barriers). Thus, strategic isolation can be a more general approach for those who aspire to exploit the mistakes of others.

Overall, this discussion suggests that a strategist should reduce dependency before exploiting a behavioral opportunity by translating under- or overvalued resources into unambiguous superior performances, searching for opportunities in remote networks where local interdependency is strong for insiders but weak for the strategist, reducing exposure to potentially biased information and evaluators.

How to learn more effectively than others

To overcome learning barriers, a strategist can conduct counterfactual experiments to avoid being fooled by misleading data. For example, high performers can continue performing better due to strong self-reinforcing mechanisms rather than due to high or improved competence. One way to test this alternative hypothesis is to remove the resources available to high-level performers (or give the inferior performer a second chance) and examine how performances change. This does not mean that high-level performers should be punished or that low-level performers should be rewarded. The point is that statistical regression, as well as misestimations, cannot be detected or falsified if the observations are misleading unless an experiment is conducted that disentangles the confounding variables. To disentangle self-fulfilling prophecies from skill explanations, a strategist can either abstain from giving extra resources to better-performing people or give resources to those who perform poorly. By observing the outcome and comparing them with a control condition in which people who do well are given extra resources, decision-makers can estimate the role of skills and self-fulfilling prophecies. Such experimentation is costly but may generate non-intuitive insights that can overcome learning barriers.

More generally, overcoming learning barriers usually requires a strategist to have access to superior data relative to his or her rivals. The estimation can be self-defeating if the data are already contaminated by self-fulfilling or selection processes. Strategists who aspire to exploit the mistakes of others should start looking for contexts in which acquiring superior data relative to rivals is feasible. For instance, the insurance giant Progressive collected more than eleven categories of age information (among other details) in order to refine their proprietary pricing algorithm (Porter and Siggelkow 1997). As a result, they were able to quote individualized and customized premiums by differentiating in a fine-grained manner according to the risk profile of each individual. Such a deliberate attempt to acquire more data was seen as one of the crucial reasons behind their rapid rise in the 1980s in the non-standard segment of the auto insurance industry.

Nevertheless, data availability per se is not necessarily associated with attractive behavioral opportunities. If a large volume of data is available to many, behavioral opportunities are unlikely to persist because many strategists can identify and take advantage of them. Behavioral opportunities are more likely to persist in settings with limited data and where the presence of many confounding variables makes it challenging to accurately estimate the magnitude of regression to the mean. Overall, this suggests that the advantage of sophisticated strategists is greatest in moderately complex environments where acquiring data and effective learning is difficult but not impossible (Schoemaker 1990). Fortune favors the strategists who can creatively collect and analyze the data in order to see what others fail to see.

Since access to superior data is not always within a strategist's control, an alternative way to search for attractive behavioral opportunities is to focus on non-intuitive phenomena. For example, the less-is-more effects are more counterintuitive because they go against people's commonsense inferences of monotonicity. Searching for non-monotonic kinks can lead to more promising opportunities because others expect them the least. Strategists can collect consecutive performance data, measure the context-dependent regression effects, and identify whether the effects are strong enough to generate non-monotonic performance associations. For example, a less-is-more effect is more likely to occur in smaller industries (where a smaller sample size implies greater unreliability in performances), more volatile industries (where performances are more sensitive to factors beyond managers' control), and more complex industries (where interdependent systems are more sensitive to small shocks). To laypersons, non-monotonicity is counterintuitive, and therefore, they are more likely to invent causal explanations for why a less-is-more effect occurs. Strategists can then search for the contexts in which these false explanations imply flawed and consequential mistakes. Finally, strategists can also recruit and work with the naïve (March 1991): outsiders who are not aware of potentially suboptimal decision heuristics or colorful but misleading stories of why performances are regressive.

Overall, this discussion suggests that a strategist can overcome learning barriers more effectively than rivals by conducting counterfactual experiments, acquiring superior data in moderately complex environments, and focusing on unintuitive phenomena.

4.5 Summary: the context-dependent luck biases and their exploitation strategies

It is important to point out that the luck biases, the behavioral barriers, and the associated strategies to overcome them are interrelated. For example, hiring the naïve can help identify an exploitable bias and remove both barriers: These outsiders are less likely to be aware of the conventional wisdom and social norms of a given context, so they are more likely to identify, learn about, and act upon a potential luck bias. While these behavioral barriers are not mutually exclusive, each of these two barriers is built upon a distinct body of literature. For instance, searching for behavioral opportunities starts with identifying a particular bias, and this is largely informed by the behavioral decision theory literature (Kahneman et al. 1982); the learning barriers are based on the organizational learning literature (Cyert and March 1963); the interdependency barriers originate from ideas around coordination, conformity, and social evaluation in institution theory (Asch 1951; Correll et al. 2017; Oliver 1991; Zuckerman 2012). Even though these related ideas come from distinct socio-cognitive disciplines, they collectively constitute a coherent behavioral framework for competitive advantage.

While this theory is context-independent, its application has to be context-dependent. That is, a strategist needs to understand the nuances of how behavioral forces operate and interact in a specific context. Also, this theory operates across different levels of analysis. The barriers discussed can be applied to decisions by an individual or organization (e.g., failure of learning regression to the mean), but they can be between individuals and organizations (e.g., failure of coordinating with stakeholders when pursuing a unique resource). These behavioral forces together determine how attractive a behavioral opportunity is.

Figure 4.4 presents a decision flowchart in order to evaluate when an opportunity based on a bias (such as the misattribution of luck) is attractive and the strategies one can pursue to overcome the behavioral barriers mentioned above. I am not arguing that strategists should always pursue behavioral opportunities; whether this is advisable depends on a strategist's circumstances and risk appetite. Behavioral opportunities are contrarian in nature and tend to be risky: like searching for a needle in a haystack. The goal is to provide a theory of which haystacks the needle could be found, which simplifies the search but does not eliminate the risk. More generally, the ambition is to outline an alternative source of profit and opportunity for strategists to consider as an option. If a strategist wants to pursue this option, he or she should search for a potentially exploitable bias by examining how this bias can lead to systematic mispricing of strategic factors and by developing exploitation strategies. If the answer to the first question is negative, this means that behavioral opportunities may exist, although there may be no feasible strategy to exploit them.

If the answer to the first question is positive, the strategist can move on to the second step to examine whether the strategist can overcome the interdependency barrier. The opportunity is more likely to be exploited when the strategist can transform the mispriced resources into something others can value, or the strategist can position himself or herself to become less dependent on others. If the answer to the second question is negative, the interdependency barrier implies

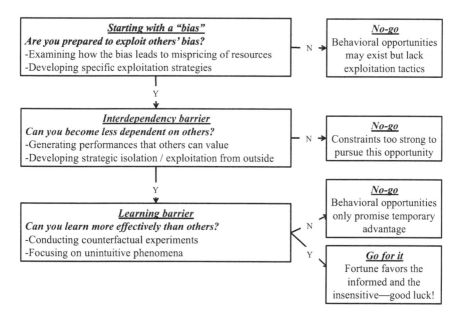

FIGURE 4.4 A decision flowchart

that the social cost may overwhelm the economic benefit of exploiting this identified opportunity for this strategist.

If the answer to the second question is positive, the strategist can examine whether he or she can overcome the learning barrier by developing counterfactual experiments. The focus should be on unintuitive phenomena, such as less-is-more effects in performance associations. If the answer to the third question is negative, the strategist may get stuck in learning traps like others or may only enjoy a short-lived advantage because others can soon learn and imitate the strategist's approaches. If the answers to all three questions are positive, it is likely that an attractive opportunity does exist and that the strategist is both analytically and socially savvy enough to identify and exploit this behavioral opportunity. Fortune favors this strategist for being informative, insightful, and insensitive.

Notes

1 Being rational here means that the person only cares about the expected payoffs measured by monetary returns.
2 My recent work extends this approach to the context of diversity and explore how prevalent discriminations create labor market inefficiencies and, in turn, profitable opportunities for the more informed.
3 The participants were recruited from a UK university ($n = 48$; 26 males and 22 females) and Amazon Mechanical Turk ($n = 157$; 85 males and 72 females). No significant differences between age and gender in the results were noticed. Therefore, I analyzed and reported the results together.
4 The second part of this chapter is adapted from my 2019 paper published in the *Academy of Management Review*, co-authored with Jerker Denrell and Christina Fang.

5

GOOD NIGHT AND GOOD LUCK

"Good night and good luck" is how controversial US journalist Edward R. Murrow would routinely sign off his 1950s television broadcasts. Given the lateness of the hour, the former is understandable but why the latter? Why is it that we wish each other good luck? Is it because however rational we may be, we remain firm in the belief that good intentions and hard work may not suffice to bring about the desired result? That our world is unpredictable?

To answer some of these questions, this book presents a perspective on the unconventional wisdom of luck. Luck can be quantified systematically, and the impact of luck can vary across different performance ranges. In particular, exceptional successes and failures usually cannot be realized without exceptional luck, making their performances most regressive in the future. On the other hand, luck can also be strategized—not because there are systematic ways of getting lucky but because the ways people mistake luck for skill is systematic. In particular, people often reward top performers and blame those who fail. I have demonstrated that this is as if one is rewarding others for their good luck and vice versa. Informed strategists can exploit other people's over- (and under-)estimation of the lucky (and unlucky) to gain an advantage.

However, the unconventional wisdom of luck is in sharp contrast to the common beliefs about luck. For example, the conventional wisdom of luck suggests that people can make their own luck or chance favor the prepared mind. Other common beliefs about luck can even be considered superstitious (e.g., many believe that there are ways to attract good luck and avoid bad luck). This final chapter of this book explores the varying beliefs about luck and aims at unpacking the possible rationality behind these seemingly irrational beliefs. This has important implications for how managers strike a balance between the conventional and the unconventional wisdom of luck.

5.1 Beliefs about luck in different cultures

How to get lucky? Or how do you avoid bad luck? Different cultures have different answers to this question. For example, you cannot find the fourth floor in most hospitals when you visit Hong Kong or Taiwan. It turns out that the pronunciation of the number 4 sounds like "death" in Chinese (including in Mandarin and several local dialects). It is a tradition in the Chinese culture to avoid anything that resonates death in contexts such as hospitals or when visiting sick friends or family members. It is believed that this will bring bad luck to them; for example, their condition will worsen. Of course, modern hospital buildings in these countries do have a fourth floor—they just call it the fifth floor (or floor 3A) to prevent "4" from being seen or mentioned. On the other hand, you may find many "8"s on car license plates when you visit countries that share the Chinese culture. The reason is that the pronunciation of "8" sounds like "making a fortune" in Chinese. People actually pay a fortune in auctions to get car license plates with many "8"s because they believe this will bring them good luck wherever they go.

Beliefs about luck exist widely in addition to the examples from the Chinese culture. In Western culture, the number 13 is usually connected to bad luck, and it is so widely held that it was given the scientific name "triskaidekaphobia." The fear of 13 is the strongest if the 13th day of a month happens to be a Friday. The origin of this belief is argued to originate from Christianity: Jesus was crucified on a Friday, and there were 13 individuals present during his last supper. Interestingly, while both the number 13 and Friday are considered unlucky, no record exists to show that the two items were construed as unlucky before the 19th century. In fact, in Spanish-speaking countries, Tuesday (instead of Friday) the 13th is considered an unlucky day; this suggests that beliefs about luck can evolve and vary even when they share the same origin. There are many other beliefs or symbols of good and bad luck. They vary so much across different cultures that they have their own Wikipedia pages (see "list of lucky symbols" and "list of bad luck signs").

Luck also plays a role in many historical turning points. Ancient cultures often saw weather as unpredictable and beyond human control and tended to account for the significant consequences resulting from the weather through luck if not destiny or divine power (Rescher 1995). For instance, changing weather conditions undeniably made significant differences to the histories of two island countries: England and Japan. England successfully fought off the invasion of the Spanish Armada in 1588, and Japan the Mongolian invasions in 1247 and 1281, with help from unpredictable weather conditions. The Spanish Armada, which means "great and most fortunate navy" in old Spanish, encountered severe weather during its invasion of England,[1] was badly damaged by the storm, and thus failed as an invasion fleet. To the English, such a result was a strong indication of luck because according to the then-comparative military power between Spain and England, England was supposed to lose mightily instead of winning convincingly. Likewise, the once-invincible Mongolian cavalry met unexpected and rough typhoons twice during their amphibious invasions of Japan and was annihilated by the Japanese on both occasions. It is no wonder that the Japanese named the typhoons, which helped them defeat the Mongolians, *Kamikaze* (the divine wind) and saw it as a symbol of luck when confronting the seemingly undefeatable enemy. This belief also concerns how the Japanese used the term *Kamikaze* during World War Two to encourage the young Japanese fighter pilots to execute suicidal missions. A lucky occasion can have enduring (and misfortunate) impacts when people over-interpret their past luck.

The term "Kokura's luck" in Japanese is another significant example of luck in history. Kokura was the primary target of the nuclear weapon *Fat Man* on 9 August 1945. However, since the city was obscured by clouds and Major Charles Sweeney of the Bockscar had specific orders to drop the bomb visually, the bombing crew moved on to Nagasaki, the secondary target, where they dropped their lethal weapon. Consequently, Kokura was a city literally saved by the clouds. Kokura's inhabitants' undeniably good luck (their narrow escape) turned out to be disastrous for Nagasaki's inhabitants (the flukish victims).

In addition to popular beliefs about luck, many academics and scientists also believe in the importance of luck in their findings and career:

> Scientists, curiously, talk a lot about luck. As murderously as they work, as dedicated as they are to rigor, as much as they may believe in their own perfection, they concede that great scientific careers are almost always favoured by something else: great timing of an unseen hand connecting the observer and the observed. Pasteur's oft-used remark about fortune encapsulates the view, almost universally shared among scientists, especially in the drug industry, that they'd rather be lucky than good.
>
> *(Werth 1994, p. 210)*

Given the ubiquity of the beliefs about luck across different cultures, including in scientific communities, are these beliefs necessarily irrational?

5.2 Can beliefs about luck be rational?

The beliefs about luck are irrational if we follow the strict definition of luck (i.e., luck as an unsystematic factor beyond humans' foresight and control). No systematic ways exist to influence the uncontrollable. Believing otherwise is to engage in an illusion of control (Langer 1975).

Nevertheless, a seemingly irrational belief may reflect an intelligent and rational adaptation process when one unpacks how such a belief emerges and persists (Denrell 2008). Consider a thought experiment: A startup founder wears a black turtleneck in an important pitch to the venture capitalists and succeeds in attracting investment. He subsequently wears the same black turtleneck in a media event, and it goes very well again. Now an interesting thought comes to his mind: Might this black turtleneck bring him good luck? Now he is attending another important corporate event: What should he wear?

This thought experiment highlights an important origin of many beliefs about luck: They are based on illusory correlations between outcomes and certain actions. The only way to verify whether the beliefs are causally valid is through falsification: examining whether the outcome would be different in the absence of the assumed cause (e.g., not wearing the black turtleneck). However, if the task structure entails an asymmetrical cost of errors, a particular belief about luck (e.g., wearing a black turtleneck brings good luck) can persist. The rationale is as follows: It may not be too costly to act based on a false belief (i.e., wearing the black turtleneck when it has nothing to do with the chance of success); however, it can be very costly not to act when the belief is actually correct (i.e., not wearing the black turtleneck when it, in fact, enhances the chance of success). When the cost of the latter is much greater than the former, it is quite rational for the startup founder to wear the black turtleneck even if he is not entirely convinced of his belief. It is simply too costly to experiment otherwise.

This approach to rationalizing human beliefs that lack scientific evidence can be traced back to the French philosopher Blaise Pascal and his famous "Pascal's Wager": A rational person should live as God exists and seek to believe in God. If God does not exist, such a person will have only a finite loss (e.g., the opportunity cost of the time spent at the church). In contrast, if God does exist, such belief will enable him or her to receive infinite gains (e.g., in Heaven for eternity) and avoid insufferable losses (e.g., in Hell for eternity). Until there is a feasible (and affordable) way to examine the existence of God, it is rational to believe that God exists because it can be too costly to believe and act otherwise.

This logic can also explain many biases regarding luck, such as how people tend to mistake luck for skill when evaluating successes and failures. For example, misjudging the causes of other people's exceptional performance can encourage explorative or riskier actions. Engaging in such actions can be useful because it can compensate for a tendency in experiential learning—one usually learns from one's own experience to bias against novel and risky alternatives (Denrell and March 2001). Furthermore, the cost of action is often relatively lower than that of inaction in competitive selection. Misjudgment can be more useful for individuals when competition is intense.

Mistaking luck for skill when evaluating exceptional performance can also be useful for a group. The misjudgment makes individual failures likely. However, such failure can bring new information to the group, particularly when other individuals in the group tend to herd together and provide little new information for the group (Bernardo and Welch 2001). A person who mistakes luck for skill when evaluating exceptional performance is more likely to engage in action. However, the costs and effects of mistaking luck for skill can vary according to the level of analysis: Individual misjudgments may, in fact, have collective, evolutionary benefits. In this sense, the long-term survival of a group can depend on a few lucky heroes who happen to achieve exceptional performance, along with many martyrs whose judgments were similar to those of the heroes, although they eventually failed (Dosi and Lovallo 1997). The heroes are likely to be more reproductively successful, with numerous offspring that carry their traits (e.g., Genghis Khan, whose lineage was found in 8% of the men in Asia, which is 0.5% of the world's population). The tendency for mistaking luck for skill when evaluating exceptional performance can, thus, be retained in human evolution (Nicolaou et al. 2008).

However, mistaking luck for skill when evaluating exceptional performance can also lead to undesirable outcomes under certain circumstances. The business media, management bestsellers, and case studies in business schools tend to focus on exceptional performance and to frame these cases as being the result of human intervention, such as superior organizational processes, leadership, or foresight (Makridakis et al. 2009; Rosenzweig 2007). These practices can lead students of exceptional performance to systematically overestimate the role of skill to such an extent that the function of misjudgments disappears.

The seemingly irrational beliefs about luck can be evolutionarily rational. However, it can become irrational when the contexts become dramatically different compared to those faced by our ancestors. Recognizing the possible mismatches is essential.

5.3 Reconciling the conventional and the unconventional wisdom of luck

The main theme of the unconventional wisdom of luck is that exceptional performances tend to occur due to exceptional luck and circumstances. However, suggesting that exceptional performance is a matter of luck poses a challenge to management researchers and educators. One can consider two necessary criteria for evaluating accounts of performance differences: accuracy and usefulness. As discussed earlier, luck can be a relatively more accurate and parsimonious account of exceptional performances. Nevertheless, this account is of limited use. Should we tell business school students who are eager to achieve high performance that they should be lucky? This may partly explain why media reports, teaching, and research focus so much on explaining luck by highlighting leadership, best practices, and superior foresight. The role of skill can be overemphasized because of its comprehensibility, pragmatic nature, ability to attract attention, and usefulness in fields such as business consultancy and education (March 2010).

I am not arguing that sacrificing accuracy for usefulness is always a bad thing. As discussed earlier, this sacrifice can lead to desirable outcomes under some circumstances. What is crucial for management researchers and educators is to understand better the tradeoff in outcomes between emphasizing usefulness (i.e., skill) and emphasizing accuracy (i.e., luck) in different contexts.

Emphasizing skill is likely to backfire in several common situations. On the one hand, most business schools tend to cater to students' demands and emphasize how to achieve high performance based on instrumental rationality. This can lead to recurring endogenous crises due to the increasing complexity of modern societies: "Technologies of rationality seem clearly to be effective instruments of exploitation in relatively simple situations . . . their ventures in more complex explorations seem often to lead to huge mistakes" (March 2006, p. 201). The recent hype surrounding artificial intelligence reinforces this cause for concern.

On the other hand, the cost of failures can be too high to allow modern organizations to emphasize how capability can trump uncertainty. If this emphasis takes place, actors can gain confidence more rapidly than competence. Costly, undesirable outcomes have been documented in areas such as major corporate decisions, complex projects, entrepreneurs' ventures, and financial crises. Bringing luck into the development of management research and education would allow for some reconciliation of the differing accounts of performance differences. Otherwise, "normal accidents" (Perrow 1984) will continue to happen, and business schools would share some responsibility with them.

To address the tension between the conventional and unconventional wisdom of luck, we need to understand a "fundamental paradox" in human behavior—the more uncertain the world becomes, the more people seek out and rely on seemingly certain solutions (Gimpl and Dakin 1984). Current education in business schools mostly entertains such demands—we successfully provide our students with linear and not necessarily simple (e.g., mathematical modeling) tools on dealing with uncertainty, which can seemingly lead to better performance. However, we need to reflect on the consequences of such an action, particularly as it has become obvious that these tools often lead to costly failures (March 2006).

Management research should also focus on prescriptive theories that can help business practitioners move from "incompetent to OK" rather than focusing on those that address how to move from "good to great." Current prescriptive theories of management and many business management bestsellers focus on the latter, although being "great" in business (i.e., achieving exceptional performance) is often primarily a matter of luck.

For example, many business bestsellers share a formula: selecting a few successful firms that beat the odds and achieve excellence, analyzing the shared practices of these firms when they move from good to great, and framing these practices as the benchmark for those who aspire to become great. An overlooked caveat is that the greatness featured in these bestsellers does not last. Take the 50 firms featured in the three most popular business bestsellers (Collins 2001; Collins et al. 2005; Peters and Waterman 1982): 16 of them failed within five years after the book was published; 23 became mediocre as they underperformed the S&P 500 index. What happened after becoming great is clearly not enduring greatness but regressing to below average (Clayman 1987).

This finding—from good to great to below average—should not be surprising mainly because above a certain level, no rule exists for achieving exceptional performance (Levy 2003). Achieving exceptional performance usually requires doing something different or novel, and there can be no recipe for such

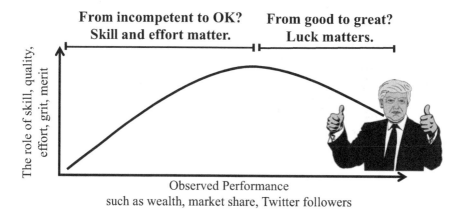

FIGURE 5.1 A graphical summary of the unconventional wisdom of luck

innovation. When they happen to succeed, many of these successes will not be sustainable but regress considerably to the mean. Students who focus on how to move from "good to great" and ignore how they regress to below average can be gaining confidence rather than competence. This follows that management research and education should focus on teaching business practitioners what to do to move from "incompetent to OK." We need to balance the accounts of exceptional performance; in other words, we need to integrate the role of luck into the development of management research and education. We also need to consider modifying the teaching we provide to our students to ensure they have the most comprehensive picture and the best possible opportunities for the future.

Figure 5.1 provides a useful summary of fending off the intuition that exceptional performers are better. Higher performers are likely better, and the key for a poor, novice performer to become a good, experienced one is not about luck but skill and effort. The conventional wisdom of luck, such as "the harder I work, the luckier I get" or "chance favors the prepared mind," makes perfect sense when one focuses on moderate performance. Moving from good to great, however, is a different story. Being at the right place (e.g., succeeding in a context where early outcomes have enduring impacts) and at the right time (e.g., having early luck or a large endowment) can be so important that it overwhelms merits.

With this in mind, there is a good case that we should not just reward or imitate life's winners and expect to repeat their successes. That said, there is a case that winners should consider imitating the likes of Gates (who became a philanthropist) or Warren Buffett (who argues that richer Americans should pay higher taxes), who have chosen to commit their wealth and success to worthy causes. The winners who appreciate their luck and do not take it all for themselves deserve a larger portion of our respect.

Note

1 Many myths surround the Spanish Armada. One of them is that the English fleet led by Sir Francis Drake used long-range artillery to defeat the Spanish Armada. In fact, few of the Armada battleships were sunk by the English. This myth of Drake's military superiority intentionally presented by the English writers as a pivotal moment in European history ignores the fact that this battle actually marked the beginning of an increase in Spanish naval supremacy rather than a long decline.

ACKNOWLEDGMENTS

Many friends and colleagues asked me why I chose to study the topic of luck. I did not really have a good answer to their question until I wrote this book: I chose this topic because it is fun, and there was no competition when I started my Ph.D. in Cambridge in autumn 2007! Some scholars have studied this topic outside management; however, almost none exists in management. After I started teaching strategy courses, I realized that this was as if I had applied a Blue Ocean Strategy (Kim and Mauborgne 2014:1): "creating and capturing uncontested market space, thereby making the competition irrelevant."

As the theme of the unconventional wisdom of luck suggests, the fact that I can write a book to summarize my ten-year research on luck indicates that I was extremely lucky. In many plausible counterfactual scenarios, I could have failed terribly when adopting such a contrarian approach: My destination would not have been a blue ocean but a deadly desert (not even a hypercompetitive, red ocean). Of course, I do not mind taking some credit for my own effort and persistence. However, the following should take more credit in allowing me to be in a fortunate position to complete this book.

My lovely wife, Mandy, should take much credit for making this book possible. Procrastination hit me on several occasions after starting this book: There are always "more urgent" things to deal with, such as meeting revision deadlines, delivering executive education, or watching the latest anime (yes, I am still a fan . . .). Eventually, she could no longer stand it and asked me to bring my computer during our vacations—I was not allowed to enjoy myself until after making significant progress on the chapters of this book (judged by her, of course). I can still feel those hard-working evenings in Venice, Kathmandu, Taipei, etc. when reading through parts of the book now. I thank Mandy for pushing me to my limit!

I would also like to thank my mentor and research partner, Jerker Denrell. Jerker's work attracted my attention from the beginning of my doctoral study.

He is *the* management scholar who studied luck then. We first met at a conference in Anaheim, where I also met his mentor, Jim March. Their feedback on my (very immature) research encouraged me greatly. Jerker moved from Stanford to Oxford in 2009, which I consider being the luckiest event in the development of my research career. He enlightened me on how to extend my research on luck, and his comments on my research substantially strengthened my Ph.D. thesis. We have co-authored more than ten papers in the past ten years, and I could not envision any better counterfactual scenario other than developing my academic career under his mentorship. Chapters 3 and 4 were also partly based on our co-authored papers. I thank Jerker for guiding me to become a scholar!

I would also like to thank my research partner, Christina Fang, and my Ph.D. advisor, Mark de Rond, who were the co-authors of Chapters 4 and 2, respectively. I am grateful for their support for my research program and the publication of this book. I also thank the following colleagues, who commented on the earlier version of the chapters (order is determined by luck of the draw): Loizos Heracleous, Dan Levinthal, Anne Miner, Daniel Read, Nick Chater, Christian Stadler, Thomas Powell, Jim March, Phanish Puranam, Balazs Kovacs, Thorbjorn Knudsen, Kiersten Burge-Hendrix, Brian Burge-Hendrix, Tobias Gerstenberg, Rueylin Hsiao, Freek Vermeulen, and Don Lange. Their feedback sharpened my ideas and the book substantially.

I acknowledge the generous financial support from Warwick Business School, ESMT Berlin, and the Taiwanese Overseas Pioneers Grants. I also thank the *Academy of Management Review* and *Academy of Management Annals* for allowing me to use part of my papers published in their journals in this book.

Finally, I would like to thank Terry Clague at Routledge, who encouraged me to write this book and was incredibly supportive when my father passed away unexpectedly shortly after I started the book.

I dedicate this book to my wonderful parents with love and gratitude.

Chengwei Liu
London, England
August 2019

REFERENCES

Akerlof, G.A., Shiller, R.J. (2015) *Phishing for Phools: The Economics of Manipulation and Deception* (Princeton University Press, Princeton, NJ).

Alchian, A. (1950) Uncertainty, evolution, and economic theory. *Journal of Political Economy* 58(3):211–221.

Alesina, A., Glaeser, E., Sacerdote, B. (2001) Why doesn't the US have a European-style welfare system? *Brookings Papers on Economic Activity* 3(1):1–66.

Alvesson, M., Sandberg, J. (2011) Generating research questions through problematization. *Academy of Management Review* 36(2):247–271.

Andriani, P., Cattani, G. (2016) Exaptation as source of creativity, innovation, and diversity: Introduction to the special section. *Industrial and Corporate Change* 25(1):115–131.

Arendt, H. (1963) *Eichmann in Jerusalem* (Penguin, London, UK).

Argote, L., Epple, D. (1990) Learning curves in manufacturing. *Science* 247(4945):920–924.

Armstrong, J.S., Collopy, F. (1992) Error measures for generalizing about forecasting methods: Empirical comparisons. *International Journal of Forecasting* 8(1):69–80.

Arthur, W.B. (1989) Competing technologies, increasing returns, and lock-in by historical events. *The Economic Journal* 99(394):116–131.

Asch, S.E. (1951) Effects of group pressure upon the modification and distortion of judgments. Guetzkow, H., ed. *Groups, Leadership, and Men* (Carnegie Press, Pittsburgh, PA), 222–236.

Audia, P.G., Locke, E.A., Smith, K.G. (2000) The paradox of success: An archival and a laboratory study of strategic persistence following radical environmental change. *Academy of Management Journal* 43(5):837–853.

Austin, J.H. (1978) *Chase, Chance, and Creativity: The Lucky Art of Novelty* (Columbia University Press, New York, NY).

Ayton, P., Fischer, I. (2004) The hot hand fallacy and the gambler's fallacy: Two faces of subjective randomness? *Memory & Cognition* 32(8):1369–1378.

Barabasi, A.L., Albert, R. (1999) Emergence of scaling in random networks. *Science* 286(5439):509–512.

Barberis, N., Thaler, R. (2003) A survey of behavioral finance. *Handbook of the Economics of Finance* 1:1053–1128.

Barnett, W.P. (2008) *The Red Queen Among Organizations: How Competitiveness Evolves* (Princeton University Press, Princeton, NJ).

Barney, J. (1991) Firm resources and sustained competitive advantage. *Journal of Management* 17(1):99–120.

Barney, J.B. (1986) Strategic factor markets: Expectations, luck, and business strategy. *Management Science* 32(10):1231–1241.

Barney, J.B. (1997) On flipping coins and making technology decisions: Luck on an explanation of technological foresight and oversight. Garud, R., Nayyar, P.R., Shapira, Z.B., eds. *Technological Innovation Oversights and Foresights* (Cambridge University Press, New York, NY), 13–19.

Barney, J.B. (2018) Why resource-based theory's model of profit appropriation must incorporate a stakeholder perspective. *Strategic Management Journal* in press, available on-line.

Barnsley, R.H., Thompson, A.H., Barnsley, P.E. (1985) Hockey success and birthdate: The relative age effect. *Canadian Association for Health, Physical Education, and Recreation Journal* 51(1):23–28.

Baron, J., Hershey, J.C. (1988) Outcome bias in decision evaluation. *Journal of Personality and Social Psychology* 54(4):569–579.

Bearden, J.N., Wallsten, T.S., Fox, C.R. (2007) Contrasting stochastic and support theory accounts of subadditivity. *Journal of Mathematical Psychology* 51(4):229–241.

Beaver, W.H. (1968) The information content of annual earnings announcements. *Journal of Accounting Research* 19(1):67–92.

Bebchuk, L.A., Fried, J.M. (2009) *Pay without Performance: The Unfulfilled Promise of Executive Compensation* (Harvard University Press, Cambridge, MA).

Benabou, R., Tirole, J. (2006) Belief in a just world and redistributive politics. *Quarterly Journal of Economics* 121(2):699–746.

Benner, M.J., Zenger, T. (2016) The lemons problem in markets for strategy. *Strategy Science* 1(2):71–89.

Bernardo, A.E., Welch, I. (2001) On the evolution of overconfidence and entrepreneurs. *Journal of Economics & Management Strategy* 10(3):301–330.

Bertrand, M., Mullainathan, S. (2001) Are CEOs rewarded for Luck? The ones without principals are. *Quarterly Journal of Economics* 116(3):901–932.

Boeker, W. (1992) Power and managerial dismissal: Scapegoating at the top. *Administrative Science Quarterly* 37(3):400–421.

Burgelman, R.A. (2003) Practice and you get luckier. *European Business Forum* 1(16):38–39.

Byrne, R. (2005) *The Rational Imagination: How People Create Alternatives to Reality* (MIT Press, Cambridge, MA).

Camerer, C.F., Ho, T.H., Chong, J.K. (2004) A cognitive hierarchy model of games. *The Quarterly Journal of Economics* 119(3):861–898.

Carroll, G.R., Harrison, J.R. (1994) On the historical efficiency of competition between organizational populations. *American Journal of Sociology* 100(3):720–749.

Cattani, G. (2005) Preadaptation, firm heterogeneity, and technological performance: A study on the evolution of fiber optics, 1970–1995. *Organization Science* 16(6):563–580.

Christensen, C.M. (1997) *The Innovator's Dilemma: When New Technologies Cause Great Firms to Fail* (Harvard Business School Press, Cambridge, MA).

Clayman, M. (1987) In search of excellence: The investor's viewpoint. *Financial Analysts Journal* 43(3):54–63.

Coad, A. (2009) *The Growth of Firms: A Survey of Theories and Empirical Evidence* (Edward Elgar Publishing, Cheltenham, UK).

Cockburn, I.M., Henderson, R.M., Stern, S. (2000) Untangling the origins of competitive advantage. *Strategic Management Journal*: 1123–1145.

Cohen, M.D., March, J.G., Olsen, J.P. (1972) A garbage can model of organizational choice. *Administrative Science Quarterly* 17(1):1–25.

Cohen, W.M., Levinthal, D.A. (1990) Absorptive capacity: A new perspective on learning and innovation. *Administrative Science Quarterly* 35(1):128–152.

Collins, J., Hansen, M.T. (2011) *Great by Choice: Uncertainty, Chaos and Luck-Why Some Thrive despite Them All* (Random House, London, UK).

Collins, J.C. (2001) *Good to Great: Why Some Companies Make the Leap- and Others Don't* (Harper, New York, NY).

Collins, J.C., Collins, J., Porras, J.I. (2005) *Built to Last: Successful Habits of Visionary Companies* (Random House, New York, NY).

Cornelissen, J., Durand, R. (2012) More than just novelty: Conceptual blending and causality. *Academy of Management Review* 37(1):152–154.

Correll, S.J., Ridgeway, C.L., Zuckerman, E.W., Jank, S. (2017) It's the conventional thought that counts: How third-order inference produces status advantage. *American Sociological Review* 82(2):297–327.

Coughlan, A.T., Schmidt, R. (1985) Executive compensation, management turnover, and firm performance. *Journal of Accounting and Economics* 7(1–3):43–66.

Cowley, R. (2002) *What If?* (Penguin, London, UK).

Cyert, R.M., March, J.G. (1963) *A Behavioral Theory of the Firm* (Blackwell Publishers Inc., Malden, MA).

Darke, P.R., Freedman, J.L. (1997) The belief in good luck scale. *Journal of Research in Personality* 31:481–511.

David, P.A. (1985) Clio and the economics of QWERTY. *American Economic Review* 75(2):332–337.

De Bondt, W.F., Thaler, R. (1985) Does the stock market overreact? *The Journal of Finance* 40(3):793–805.

Delong, J.B., Shleifer, A., Summers, L.H., Waldmann, R.J. (1990) Noise trader risk in financial-markets. *Journal of Political Economy* 98(4):703–738.

Denis, D.J., Kruse, T.A. (2000) Managerial discipline and corporate restructuring following performance declines. *Journal of Financial Economics* 55(3):391–424.

Denrell, J. (2003) Vicarious learning, undersampling of failure, and the myths of management. *Organization Science* 14(3):227–243.

Denrell, J. (2004) Random walks and sustained competitive advantage. *Management Science* 50(7):922–934.

Denrell, J. (2005) Why most people disapprove of me: Experience sampling in impression formation. *Psychological Review* 112(4):951–978.

Denrell, J. (2008) Superstitious behavior as a byproduct of intelligent adaptation. Starbuck, W., Hodkinson, G., eds. *Handbook of Organizational Decision Making* (Oxford University Press, Oxford).

Denrell, J., Fang, C. (2010) Predicting the next big thing: Success as a signal of poor judgment. *Management Science* 56(10):1653–1667.

Denrell, J., Fang, C., Liu, C. (2015) Chance explanations in the management sciences. *Organization Science* 26(3):923–940.

Denrell, J., Fang, C., Liu, C. (2019) In search of behavioral opportunities from misattributions of luck. *Academy of Management Review* 44(4):896-915.

Denrell, J., Fang, C., Winter, S.G. (2003) The economics of strategic opportunity. *Strategic Management Journal* 24(10):977–990.

Denrell, J., Fang, C., Zhao, Z. (2013) Inferring superior capabilities from sustained superior performance: A Bayesian analysis. *Strategic Management Journal* 34(2):182–196.

Denrell, J., Liu, C. (2012) Top performers are not the most impressive when extreme performance indicates unreliability. *Proceedings of the National Academy of Sciences* 109(24):9331–9336.

Denrell, J., Liu, C., Le Mens, G. (2017) When more selection is worse. *Strategy Science* 2(1):39–63.

Denrell, J., March, J.G. (2001) Adaptation as information restriction: The hot stove effect. *Organization Science* 12(5):523–538.

de Rond, M. (2014) The structure of serendipity. *Culture and Organization* 20(5):342–358.

de Rond, M., Thietart, R.A. (2007) Choice, chance, and inevitability in strategy. *Strategic Management Journal* 28(5):535–551.

Dillon, R.L., Tinsley, C.H. (2008) How near-misses influence decision making under risk: A missed opportunity for learning. *Management Science* 54(8):1425–1440.

Dorner, D. (1996) *The Logic of Failure: Recognizing and Avoiding Error in Complex Situations* (Metropolitan Books, New York, NY).

Dosi, G., Lovallo, D. (1997) Rational entrepreneurs or optimistic martyrs? Some considerations on technological regimes, corporate entries, and the evolutionary role of decision biases. Garud, R., Nayyar, P.R., Shapira, Z.B., eds. *Technological Innovation: Oversights and Foresights* (Cambridge University Press, New York).

Durand, R., Vaara, E. (2009) Causation, counterfactuals and competitive advantage. *Strategic Management Journal* 30(12):1245–1264.

Dye, K.C., Eggers, J.P., Shapira, Z. (2014) Trade-offs in a tempest: Stakeholder influence on hurricane evacuation decisions. *Organization Science* 25(4):1009–1025.

Elberse, A. (2013) *Blockbusters: Hit-Making, Risk-Taking, and the Big Business of Entertainment* (Macmillan, New York, NY).

Faisal, A.A., Selen, L.P., Wolpert, D.M. (2008) Noise in the nervous system. *Nature Reviews Neuroscience* 9(4):292–303.

Fama, E.F. (1980) Agency problems and the theory of the firm. *The Journal of Political Economy* 88(2):288–307.

Fama, E.F., French, K.R. (2010) Luck versus skill in the cross-section of mutual fund returns. *The Journal of Finance* 65(5):1915–1947.

Feldman, J.M. (1981) Beyond attribution theory: Cognitive processes in performance appraisal. *Journal of Applied Psychology* 66(2):127–148.

Feller, W. (1968) *An Introduction to Probability Theory and its Applications*, Vol. 2 (Wiley, New York, NY).

Fildes, R., Goodwin, P., Lawrence, M., Nikolopoulos, K. (2009) Effective forecasting and judgmental adjustments: An empirical evaluation and strategies for improvement in supply-chain planning. *International Journal of Forecasting* 25(1):3–23.

Fischhoff, B. (1975) Hindsight not equal to foresight: Effect of outcome knowledge on judgment under uncertainty. *Journal of Experimental Psychology-Human Perception and Performance* 1(3):288–299.

Fischhoff, B., Slovic, P., Lichtenstein, S. (1978) Fault trees: Sensitivity of estimated failure probabilities to problem representation. *Journal of Experimental Psychology: Human Perception and Performance* 4(2):330–344.

Fiske, S.T., Taylor, S.E. (2013) *Social Cognition: From Brains to Culture* (Sage, New York, NY).

Fitza, M.A. (2014) The use of variance decomposition in the investigation of CEO effects: How large must the CEO effect be to rule out chance? *Strategic Management Journal* 35(12):1839–1852.

Fox, C.R., Rogers, B.A., Tversky, A. (1996) Options traders exhibit subadditive decision weights. *Journal of Risk and Uncertainty* 13(1):5–17.

Frank, R.H. (2016) *Success and Luck: Good Fortune and the Myth of Meritocracy* (Princeton University Press, Princeton, NJ).

Gavetti, G. (2012) Toward a behavioral theory of strategy. *Organization Science* 23(1):267–285.

Geroski, P.A. (2005) Understanding the implications of empirical work on corporate growth rates. *Managerial and Decision Economics* 26(2):129–138.

Gilbert, D.T., Malone, P.S. (1995) The correspondence bias. *Psychological Bulletin* 117(1):21–38.

Gimpl, M.L., Dakin, S.R. (1984) Management and magic. *California Management Review* 27(1):125–136.

Gladwell, M. (2008) *Outliers: The Story of Success* (Allen Lane, London, UK).

Gould, R.V. (2002) The origins of status hierarchies: A formal theory and empirical test. *American Journal of Sociology* 107(5):1143–1178.

Greve, H.R. (1999) The effect of core change on performance: Inertia and regression toward the mean. *Administrative Science Quarterly* 44(3):590–614.

Greve, H.R. (2003) *Organizational Learning from Performance Feedback: A Behavioral Perspective on Innovation and Change* (Cambridge University Press, Cambridge, England).

Gromet, D.M., Hartson, K.A., Sherman, D.K. (2015) The politics of luck: Political ideology and the perceived relationship between luck and success. *Journal of Experimental Social Psychology* 59:40–46.

Groysberg, B. (2010) *Chasing Stars: The Myth of Talent and the Portability of Performance* (Princeton University Press, Princeton, NJ).

Groysberg, B., Nanda, A., Nohria, N. (2004) The risky business of hiring stars. *Harvard Business Review* 82(5):92–101.

Hambrick, D.C., Finkelstein, S. (1987) Managerial discretion: A bridge between polar views of organizational outcomes. *Research in Organizational Behavior* 9(1):369–406.

Hannan, M.T., Freeman, J. (1984) Structural inertia and organizational change. *American Sociological Review* 49(2):149–164.

Hannan, M.T., Freeman, J. (1989) *Organizational Ecology* (Harvard University Press, Cambridge, MA).

Harrison, J.R., March, J.G. (1984) Decision making and postdecision surprises. *Administrative Science Quarterly* 29(1):26–42.

Helfat, C.E., Finkelstein, S., Mitchell, W., Peteraf, M., Singh, H., Teece, D., Winter, S.G. (2007) *Dynamic Capabilities: Understanding Strategic Change in Organizations* (Blackwell, Oxford).

Herndon, T., Ash, M., Pollin, R. (2014) Does high public debt consistently stifle economic growth? A critique of Reinhart and Rogoff. *Cambridge Journal of Economics* 38(2):257–279.

Hertwig, R., Barron, G., Weber, E.U., Erev, I. (2004) Decisions from experience and the effect of rare events in risky choice. *Psychological Science* 15(8):534–539.

Hewstone, M. (1989) *Causal Attribution: From Cognitive Processes to Collective Beliefs* (Wiley-Blackwell, London, UK).

Hilbert, M. (2012) Toward a synthesis of cognitive biases: How noisy information processing can bias human decision making. *Psychological Bulletin* 138(2):1–27.

Hogarth, R.M. (2001) *Educating Intuition* (University of Chicago Press, Chicago, IL).

Hotelling, H. (1933) Book review: The triumph of mediocrity in business. *Journal of the American Statistical Association* 28(184):463–465.

Jensen, M.C., Meckling, W.H. (1976) Theory of the firm: Managerial behavior, agency costs, and ownership structure. *Journal of Financial Economics* 3(4):305–360.

Jordan, A.H., Audia, P.G. (2012) Self-enhancement and learning from performance feed-back. *Academy of Management Review* 37(2):211–231.

Kahneman, D. (2011) *Thinking, Fast and Slow* (Penguin, London, UK).

Kahneman, D., Lovallo, D. (1993) Timid choices and bold forecasts: A cognitive perspective on risk taking. *Management Science* 39(1):17–31.

Kahneman, D., Miller, D.T. (1986) Norm theory: Comparing reality to its alternatives. *Psychological Review* 93(2):136–153.

Kahneman, D., Slovic, P., Tversky, A. (1982) *Judgment under Uncertainty: Heuristics and Biases* (Cambridge University Press, New York, NY).

Kahneman, D., Tversky, A. (1973) On the psychology of prediction. *Psychological Review* 80(4):237–251.

Kelley, H.H. (1971) *Attribution in Social Interaction* (General Learning Corporation, New York, NY).

Khurana, R. (2002) *Searching for a Corporate Savior: The Irrational Quest for Charismatic CEOs* (Princeton University Press, Princeton, NJ).

Kim, W.C., Mauborgne, R.A. (2014) *Blue Ocean Strategy, Expanded Edition: How to Create Uncontested Market Space and Make the Competition Irrelevant* (Harvard Business Review Press, Brighton, MA).

Langer, E.J. (1975) Illusion of control. *Journal of Personality and Social Psychology* 32(2):311–328.

Lee, J., Boatwright, P., Kamakura, W.A. (2003) A Bayesian model for prelaunch sales forecasting of recorded music. *Management Science* 49(2):179–196.

Levinthal, D.A. (1991) Random walks and organizational mortality. *Administrative Science Quarterly* 36(3):397–420.

Levinthal, D.A., March, J.G. (1993) The myopia of learning. *Strategic Management Journal* 14(8):95–112.

Levitt, B., March, J.G. (1988) Organizational learning. *Annual Review of Sociology* 14:319–340.

Levitt, B., Nass, C. (1989) The lid on the garbage can: Institutional constraints on decision making in the technical core of college-text publishers. *Administrative Science Quarterly* 34(2):190–207.

Levy, M. (2003) Are rich people smarter? *Journal of Economic Theory* 110(1):42–64.

Lewis, M. (2003) *Moneyball: The Art of Winning an Unfair Game* (WW Norton & Company, New York, NY).

Lewis, M. (2011) *The Big Short: Inside the Doomsday Machine* (WW Norton & Company, New York, NY).

Lieberman, M.B., Montgomery, D.B. (1988) 1st-mover Advantages. *Strategic Management Journal* 9:41–58.

Lippman, S.A., Rumelt, R.P. (1982) Uncertain imitability: An analysis of interfirm differences in efficiency under competition. *The Bell Journal of Economics* 13(2):418–438.

Litov, L.P., Moreton, P., Zenger, T.R. (2012) Corporate strategy, analyst coverage, and the uniqueness paradox. *Management Science* 58(10):1797–1815.

Liu, C., de Rond, M. (2016) Good night and good luck: Perspectives on luck in management scholarship. *Academy of Management Annals* 10(1):409–451.

Liu, C., Eubanks, D., Chater, N. (2015) Weakness of strong ties: Decision biases, social ties and nepotism in family business succession. *Leadership Quarterly* 26(1):419–435.

Liu, C., Vlaev, I., Fang, C., Denrell, J., Chater, N. (2017) Strategizing with biases: Engineering choice contexts for better decisions using the Mindspace approach. *California Management Review* 59(3):135–161.

Lynn, F.B., Podolny, J.M., Tao, L. (2009) A sociological (de)construction of the relationship between status and quality. *American Journal of Sociology* 115(3):755–804.

Makridakis, S., Hogarth, R., Gaba, A. (2009) *Dance with Chance: Making Luck Work for You* (Oneworld, London, UK).

Maltby, J., Day, L., Gill, P., Colley, A., Wood, A.M. (2008) Beliefs around luck: Confirming the empirical conceptualization of beliefs around luck and the development of the Darke and Freedman beliefs around luck scale. *Personality and Individual Differences* 45(7):655–660.

March, J.C., March, J.G. (1977) Almost random careers: The Wisconsin school superintendency, 1940–1972. *Administrative Science Quarterly* 22(3):377–409.

March, J.G. (1991) Exploration and exploitation in organizational learning. *Organization Science* 2(1):71–87.

March, J.G. (2006) Rationality, foolishness, and adaptive intelligence. *Strategic Management Journal* 27(3):201–214.

March, J.G. (2010) *The Ambiguities of Experience* (Cornell University Press, Ithaca, NY).

March, J.G., Sproull, L.S., Tamuz, M. (1991) Learning from samples of one or fewer. *Organization Science* 2(1):1–13.

Mauboussin, M.J. (2012) *The Success Equation: Untangling Skill and Luck in Business, Sports and Investing* (Harvard Business School Press, Cambridge, MA).

Meindl, J.R., Ehrlich, S.B., Dukerich, J.M. (1985) The romance of leadership. *Administrative Science Quarterly* 30(1):78–102.

Merton, R.K. (1948) The self-fulfilling prophecy. *The Antioch Review* 8(2):193–210.

Merton, R.K. (1968) The Matthew effect in science: The reward and communication systems of science. *Science* 159(3810):55–63.

Merton, R.K., Barber, E. (2006) *The Travels and Adventures of Serendipity: A Study in Sociological Semantics and the Sociology of Science* (Princeton University Press, Princeton, NJ).

Milgrom, P.R. (1981) Good news and bad news: Representation theorems and applications. *The Bell Journal of Economics* 12(2):380–391.

Miller, D.T., Ross, M. (1975) Self-serving biases in the attribution of causality: Fact or fiction? *Psychological Bulletin* 82(2):213–225.

Mintzberg, H. (1996) Learning I, planning O. *California Management Review* 38(4):92.

Mintzberg, H., Waters, J.A. (1985) Of strategies, deliberate and emergent. *Strategic Management Journal* 6(3):257–272.

Musch, J., Grondin, S. (2001) Unequal competition as an impediment to personal development: A review of the relative age effect in sport. *Developmental Review* 21(2):147–167.

Nagel, T. (1976). Moral luck. *Proceedings of the Aristotelian Society* 76(1):136–150.

Nelson, F., Winter, S. (1982) *An Evolutionary Theory of Economic Change* (Harvard University Press, Cambridge, MA).

Neri, P. (2010) How inherently noisy is human sensory processing? *Psychonomic Bulletin & Review* 17(6):802–808.

Nicolaou, N., Shane, S., Cherkas, L., Hunkin, J., Spector, T.D. (2008) Is the tendency to engage in entrepreneurship genetic? *Management Science* 54(1):167–179.

Nisbett, R.E., Ross, L. (1980) *Human Inferences: Strategies and Shortcomings of Social Judgments* (Prentice-Hall, Upper Saddle River, NJ).

Oliver, C. (1991) Strategic responses to institutional processes. *Academy of Management Review* 16(1):145–179.

Oliver, C. (1997) Sustainable competitive advantage: Combining institutional and resource-based views. *Strategic Management Journal*:697–713.

Page, S.E. (2006) Path dependence. *Quarterly Journal of Political Science* 1(1):87–115.

Perrow, C. (1984) *Normal Accidents: Living with High Risk Technologies* (Basic Books, New York, NY).

Peteraf, M.A. (1993) The cornerstones of competitive advantage: A resource-based view. *Strategic Management Journal* 14(3):179–191.

Peters, T.J., Waterman, R.H. (1982) *In Search of Excellence: Lessons from America's Best-Run Companies* (Harper, London, UK).

Pfeffer, J., Salancik, G. (1978) *The External Control of Organizations* (Harper, New York, NY).

Pierson, K., Addona, V., Yates, P. (2014) A behavioural dynamic model of the relative age effect. *Journal of Sports Sciences* 32(8):776–784.

Piketty, T. (2014) *Capital in the Twenty-First Century* (Harvard University Press, Cambridge, MA).

Pizarro, D., Uhlmann, E., Salovey, P. (2003) Asymmetry in judgments of moral blame and praise: The role of perceived metadesires. *Psychological Science* 14(3):267–272.

Pontikes, E.G., Barnett, W.P. (2017) The non-consensus entrepreneur organizational responses to vital events. *Administrative Science Quarterly* 62(1):140–178.

Porter, M.E. (1980) *Competitive Strategies: Techniques for Analyzing Industries and Competitors* (Free Press, New York, NY).

Porter, M.E. (1991) Toward a dynamic theory of strategy. *Strategic Management Journal* 12(S2):95–117.

Porter, M.E. (1996) What Is Strategy? *Harvard Business Review* 74(6):61–78.

Porter, M.E., Siggelkow, N. (1997) *Progressive Corp: HBS Case 797109* (Harvard Business Publishing, Boston, MA).

Powell, T.C. (2003) Varieties of competitive parity. *Strategic Management Journal* 24(1):61–86.

Powell, T.C., Arregle, J.L. (2007) Firm performance and the axis of errors. *Journal of Management Research* 7(2):59–77.

Pritchard, D. (2005) *Epistemic Luck* (Oxford University Press, Oxford, UK).

Reed, R., DeFillippi, R.J. (1990) Causal ambiguity, barriers to imitation, and sustainable competitive advantage. *Academy of Management Review* 15(1):88–102.

Reinhart, C.M., Rogoff, K.S. (2010) Growth in a time of debt. *American Economic Review* 100(2):573–578.

Rescher, N. (1995) *Luck: The Brilliant Randomness of Everyday Life* (University of Pittsburgh Press, Pittsburgh, PA).

Richerson, P.J., Boyd, R. (2005) *Not by Genes Alone: How Culture Transformed Human Evolution* (University of Chicago Press, Chicago, IL).

Rosenzweig, P. (2007) *The Halo Effect* (Free Press, New York, NY).

Ross, L., Nisbett, R.E. (1991) *The Person and the Situation: Perspectives of Social Psychology* (McGraw-Hill, London, UK).

Rudolph, J.W., Repenning, N.P. (2002) Disaster dynamics: Understanding the role of quantity in organizational collapse. *Administrative Science Quarterly* 47(1):1–30.

Rumelt, R. (1984) Towards a strategic theory of the firm. Lamb, R.B., ed. *Competitive Strategic Management* (Prentice Hall, Englewood Cliffs, NJ), 556–570.

Runde, J., de Rond, M. (2010) Evaluating causal explanations of specific events. *Organization Studies* 31(4):431–450.

Ryall, M.D. (2009) Causal ambiguity, complexity, and capability-based advantage. *Management Science* 55(3):389–403.

Salganik, M.J., Dodds, P.S., Watts, D.J. (2006) Experimental study of inequality and unpredictability in an artificial cultural market. *Science* 311(5762):854–856.

Samuels, M.L. (1991) Statistical reversion toward the mean: More universal than regression toward the mean. *The American Statistician* 45(4):344–346.

Samuelson, P.A. (1965) Proof that properly anticipated prices fluctuate randomly. *Industrial Management Review* 6(2):41–49.

Schmittlein, D.C. (1989) Surprising inferences from unsurprising observations: Do conditional expectations really regress to the mean? *The American Statistician* 43(3):176–183.

Schoemaker, P.J.H. (1990) Strategy, complexity and economic rent. *Management Science* 36(10):1178–1192.

Schwab, A., Abrahamson, E., Starbuck, W.H., Fidler, F. (2011) Perspective: Researchers should make thoughtful assessments instead of null-hypothesis significance tests. *Organization Science* 22(4):1105–1120.

Secrist, H. (1933) *Triumph of Mediocrity in Business* (Bureau of Business Research, Northwestern University, Chicago, IL).

Shleifer, A., Vishny, R.W. (1997) The limits of arbitrage. *Journal of Finance* 52(1):35–55.

Simonton, D.K. (2004) *Creativity in Science: Chance, Logic, Genius, and Zeitgeist* (Cambridge University Press, Cambridge, UK).

Small, M.L. (2009) *Unanticipated Gains: Origins of Network Inequality in Everyday Life: Origins of Network Inequality in Everyday Life* (Oxford University Press, Oxford, UK).

Starbuck, W.H. (1994) On behalf of naivete. Baum, J., Singh, J., eds. *Evolutionary Dynamics of Organizations* (Oxford University Press, New York, NY), 205–220.

Starbuck, W.H. (2005) How much better are the most-prestigious journals? The statistics of academic publication. *Organization Science* 16(2):180–200.

Starbuck, W.H., Farjoun, M. (2005) *Organization at the Limit: Lessons from the Columbia Disaster* (Blackwell, Malden, MA).

Stinchcombe, A.L. (1987) *Constructing Social Theories* (University of Chicago Press, Chicago).

Strang, D., Macy, M.W. (2001) In search of excellence: Fads, success stories, and adaptive emulation. *American Journal of Sociology* 107(1):147–182.

Strang, D., Patterson, K. (2014) Asymmetries in experiential and vicarious feedback: Lessons from the hiring and firing of baseball managers. *Sociological Science* 1(1):178–198.

Suchman, M.C. (1995) Managing legitimacy: Strategic and institutional approaches. *Academy of Management Review* 20(3):571–610.

Syverson, C. (2011) What determines productivity? *Journal of Economic Literature* 49(2): 326–365.

Taleb, N.N. (2001) *Fooled by Randomness: The Hidden Role of Chance in Life and in the Markets* (Penguin, London, UK).

Tetlock, P. (2005) *Expert Political Judgment: How Good Is It? How Can We Know?* (Princeton University Press, Princeton, NJ).

Tetlock, P.E., Belkin, A. (1996) *Counterfactual Thought Experiments in World Politics: Logical, Methodological, and Psychological Perspectives* (Princeton University Press, Princeton, NJ).

Thaler, R.H. (2012) *The Winner's Curse: Paradoxes and Anomalies of Economic Life* (Simon and Schuster, New York, NY).

Thaler, R.H. (2015) *Misbehaving: The Making of Behavioral Economics* (WW Norton & Company, New York, NY).

Thaler, R.H., Sunstein, C.R. (2008) *Nudge: Improving Decisions about Health, Wealth, and Happiness* (Yale University Press, New Haven, CT).

Thorngate, W., Dawes, R., Foddy, M. (2008) *Judging Merit* (Psychology Press, New York, NY).

Todd, P.M., Gigerenzer, G. (2012) *Ecological Rationality: Intelligence in the World* (Oxford University Press, Oxford, UK).

Tsang, E.W., Ellsaesser, F. (2011) How contrastive explanation facilitates theory building. *Academy of Management Review* 36(2):404–419.

Tsang, E.W.K. (2004) Toward a scientific inquiry into superstitious business decision-making. *Organization Studies* 25(6):923–946.

Tversky, A., Koehler, D.J. (1994) Support theory: A nonextensional representation of subjective probability. *Psychological Review* 101(4):547–567.

Uhlmann, E.L., Pizarro, D.A., Diermeier, D. (2015) A person-centered approach to moral judgment. *Perspectives on Psychological Science* 10(1):72–81.

Vanneste, B.S. (2017) How much do industry, corporation, and business matter, really? A meta-analysis. *Strategy Science* 2(2):121–139.

Vaughan, D. (1997) *The Challenger Launch Decision: Risky Technology, Culture, and Deviance at NASA* (University of Chicago Press, Chicago, IL).

Wang, T.V., van Loon, P., Rogier, J., Van den Assem, M.J., Van Dolder, D. (2016) Number preferences in lotteries. *Judgment and Decision Making* 11(3):243–259.

Weick, K.E., Sutcliffe, B.T. (2006) *Managing the Unexpected: Assuring High Performance in an Age of Complexity* (John Wiley & Sons, London, UK).

Weiner, B., Frieze, I., Kukla, A., Reed, L., Rest, S., Rosenbaum, R.M. (1971) *Perceiving the Cause of Success and Failure* (General Learning Press, New York, NY).

Werth, B. (1994) *The Billion Dollar Molecule: New York: Touchstone* (Simon & Schuster, New York, NY).

Wiesenfeld, B.M., Wurthmann, K.A., Hambrick, D.C. (2008) The stigmatization and devaluation of elites associated with corporate failures: A process model. *Academy of Management Review* 33(1):231–251.

Williamson, B. (1981) *Moral Luck* (Cambridge University Press, Cambridge, UK).

Young, L., Nichols, S., Saxe, R. (2010) Investigating the neural and cognitive basis of moral luck: It's not what you do but what you know. *Review of Philosophy and Psychology* 1(3):333–349.

Zuckerman, E.W. (2012) Construction, concentration, and (dis) continuities in social valuations. *Annual Review of Sociology* 38(1):223–245.

INDEX

Note: Page numbers in *italics* indicate a figure on the corresponding page.